KU-033-338

Jack Fryer studied music at the University of Durham and has been involved in teaching music for much of his career, particularly to young people. He has taken many youth orchestras on tour abroad. He became interested in Suzuki's methods in 1972, when he set up the first local authority Suzuki Teaching Scheme in Salford, a project which has grown and become firmly established. He has now left the full-time education service and is working freelance as a conductor, lecturer and adjudicator.

Jack Fryer

The Suzuki
Method

A guide for parents

Fontana/Collins

First published as *Give Your Child the Right Start*
by Souvenir Press 1985
First issued in Fontana Paperbacks 1987

Copyright © Jack Fryer 1985

Made and printed in Great Britain by
William Collins Sons & Co. Ltd, Glasgow

To Colin Green, his staff,
and all the 'Salford Suzukis'

Contents

Foreword

I feel respect and friendly feelings for everyone. In particular I cannot help but feel respect and warm friendship for small children. And my heart brims over with a desire to help make all the children born upon this earth fine human beings, happy people, people of superior ability. My whole life and energies are devoted to this end. This is because of my discovery that every single child, without exception, is born with this possibility.

People say that I am trying to do the impossible, and expanding my energies for nothing. But I know that what I conceive *is* possible, and I believe that one day the human race will create the kind of world in which everyone will realise that children have the potential.

Shinichi Suzuki
from *Nurtured by Love*
published by Exposition Press,
USA.

AUTHOR'S NOTE

In this book the masculine pronouns 'he', 'him', 'his' are used for a child of either sex merely for the sake of brevity and clarity. It should not be assumed that Suzuki pupils are all boys; on the contrary, records indicate that girls are usually in a slight majority in most classes. The talent for learning is implanted in both sexes and all races. The Suzuki concept is both international and non-sexist.

Preface

When I first began to study Shinichi Suzuki's philosophy of Talent Education and the contribution of music to a child's mental and emotional development, there were all too few facts about the system readily available in Britain. That was in 1970. Two years later, after hearing glowing reports of its success in other countries, notably the USA and Australia and, of course, in its birthplace of Japan, I organised a pilot project in co-operation with Colin Green, a teacher of the violin in Salford. There were twelve small children, plus their parents. Both he and I were delighted and amazed at the success of the scheme. From that time onwards the numbers of pupils have steadily grown.

Experience taught us that there had to be some minor modification of the method of teaching, although there was no need to ignore the basic tenets of Suzuki's own direction. The spirit of Suzuki's teaching has always been kept to the forefront. The very kernel of that spirit is the need to realise that it is never too early to foster a child's awareness of the rich variety of sight and sound which will help to develop his intelligence and zest for life. And that must come from the child's parents – long before he can harness the means of expression, be they through the ability to read and write, or to create music.

Professional advice and aid have greatly improved since the British Suzuki Institute was founded. So far, however, the number of teachers who have completed the Institute's course has remained comparatively small. The training is long and involves understanding methods which, because of their Oriental approach, are unfamiliar, although they are based on sound educational theory and practice.

Parents may find that, on average, the teachers they approach have had conventional training, but many now recognise the unique benefits of the Suzuki system and have adapted it to their own outlook. Thus their methods of musical teaching will not precisely follow the Suzuki philosophy, or all of his methods.

This need not be an obstacle to enjoying the overall benefits of the Suzuki approach. Talent Education is not founded on a rigid programme, but is flexible enough to suit the needs of both child and teacher. For example, Suzuki advocates that a parent should learn to play an instrument with her child. Even the most conscientious parent may not wish to do this, and an adaptable teacher will not insist on it.

All that is really needed is for one or both parents to give the child undivided attention and provide steady encouragement in the home environment.

The main purpose of this book is to show parents how they can understand and help to develop their children's potential—not only through music but in the general awareness of the world in which they are growing up. Every baby is born with the ability to attain the four benefits of living which Suzuki identifies as 'love, truth, virtue, and beauty'. They are gifts which can be the rewards offered by the Talent Education system.

Jack Fryer

1 A Life of Infinite Promise

A new-born baby – your baby – comes into the world with potential abilities far exceeding those of any other creature on earth.

Every parent knows this, of course. But how can all this latent array of gifts be developed so that the baby not only enjoys good health and a long life, but develops into a happy, well-rounded human being?

Wonderful as the early evidence of a baby's zest for living may be, it is not easy, merely from a mother's instinctive knowledge, to realise that all his implanted talents and qualities are not lying completely dormant but are eager to become active.

During the intervals between sleeping, the new-born baby does not merely breathe, cry, and grip with his fingers: he is already absorbing information about the world around him.

In fact, he has been doing so since well before he was born. He has been registering sounds. Weeks before birth a baby will react with shock to a violent noise, whether his mother does so or not.

Less evident to the mother is the embryo's sensitivity to gentler sounds. A psychologist, Clifford Olds, has conducted research at the Rochford maternity hospital in Essex with an ultrasonic foetal heart monitor, to investigate unborn babies' reactions to music. He found that an embryo moves away from music it dislikes and towards the source of music it finds appealing. Reactions vary according to the type of music: rock will make the embryo kick in protest; what is generally known as classical music, such as Mozart and Vivaldi, causes the embryo to move slightly within the restricted area of the womb, as if to hear it more clearly. And the baby-to-be is already developing his personal tastes. He does not always react favourably to a tune his mother enjoys.

Even more remarkable evidence of the unborn child's awareness of sound has been obtained by Dr Anthony DeCaspar at the University of North Carolina. He asked sixteen expectant mothers to read a simple children's story twice a day during the last 45 days of pregnancy.

After the babies were born Dr DeCaspar compared their responses to the story, which had by then been read to them ninety times, with another story they had never heard before, read to them by a stranger. A rubber nipple, connected to a tape recorder reproducing both stories, controlled an on-off switch. If the babies stopped sucking, indicating dislike, the tape, which had been playing one story, automatically stopped and then resumed with the other one.

The familiar story consistently proved to be the one which all the babies preferred, and they continued sucking when it was played. They could not, of course, understand the words, but they were able to recognise the pattern of sounds of the mother's voice, whereas they were wary of the other story read by someone whose voice was unfamiliar.

This book reflects the importance of sound, most easily identified in music, as the basis of the Suzuki theories on developing general talent. This evidence that music plays a vital role not merely in the formative months of early infancy, but even before birth, is therefore important.

At birth a baby's brain has all the cells it will ever have.

Growth is mainly an increase in the size of those cells and of the number of branching fibres that carry messages from one cell to another.

Within a week or ten days a baby will be able to recognise his mother by touch, smell and sound. These sensory powers evidently come first, followed closely by vision. A week-old baby is able to see differences in shapes. Jesse L. Conel has been studying brain development since the 1930s. He has shown that a baby less than a fortnight old is more interested in circular shapes than triangles.

This may sound a minor detail, of interest only to psychologists. In fact it is important as yet another piece of evidence that even a very young baby ceaselessly uses his intelligence and is exercising his powers of discrimination and judgment; he is not merely concerned with feeling cold or comfortable, hungry or satiated, secure or insecure.

A baby rapidly learns by scent to identify his mother, food and, in contrast, things that could be dangerous or unpleasant. In his early days of life it provides information he needs more accurately than sight, because his eyesight does not focus accurately at any distance from his face. But sound is accurately and acutely heard. He learns best at this stage by what he hears. Tonal differences and rhythms convey the aural messages. Actual words have at first no significance for him, although with constant repetition he will come to understand their meaning – the first steps to knowledge of language.

It is all too easy to consider a baby's physical development as the all-important factor, to the exclusion of his mental and emotional progress. 'There is plenty of time for him to learn things; for now I just want him to be happy and healthy', is a familiar comment from even the most conscientious and affectionate of mothers.

On the contrary, there is very little time – certainly as far as the baby's instinctive desire to learn is concerned. Nor can one justifiably protest that a tiny child cannot be expected to learn as quickly as he will when he is older. His capacity to absorb information is greater during the first three years of life than that of his adult parents, although he is 'starting from scratch' and he has to learn the very basics of living.

Of course, in those vital months of early life he must not be dragooned and disciplined into absorbing a torrent of information on matters which – correctly, in his view – are not yet of importance for his own development, even if adults consider them impressive evidence that the baby is abnormally brilliant and clever, with a high IQ.

The longest study of human growth has been conducted for more than half a century at the Fels Research Institute at the Antioch College in Yellow Springs, Ohio. On IQ tests, compiled to compare a child's mental age with his chronological age, the Institute has shown that the IQ figure in children can alter radically from year to year, both up and down. The tests merely reveal intelligence at a given time, and not the overall progress or lack of it. It is more sensible to accept that every normal child starts life with the potential to be bright and clever. Environment is all.

The very young child, hardly more than a baby, cannot learn if the environment in which he spends his waking hours is bereft of sights and sounds. This is the tragedy for babies who, because of physical problems affecting their health, exist lying supine in a cot in a hospital unit with little more than periodic attention to feed them, dry them, and check medical facts about temperature, respiration, and so on.

For most of these little patients, the expert care needed to ensure their survival will be fairly short, and they can soon be moved to the home environment where loving care will compensate for the early check to their mental and emotional development. Such is a baby's 'lust to learn', that most of these children rapidly make up for lost time and, within a matter of weeks, react to sights and sounds as satisfactorily as children who did not suffer this initial handicap. Indeed, there is plenty of evidence that an inborn timetable influences the late starter to race ahead. Premature babies are a typical example of this. Winston Churchill was born prematurely at seven months. Physically he remained shorter than other boys of his age; mentally he towered over them.

The ability to learn is present in every baby virtually as soon as he is born, although this may not be apparent without a little reflection. A baby learns to identify his mother's breast or the nipple of a feeding bottle as a source of nourishment; he recognises the face and hands of any adult who cares for him and comforts him; he is able to identify the sound of a familiar voice. Changes in taste, sight and sound will bring a quick reaction if they offer an experience that is strange and untested.

This ability to learn depends on memory, the use of which is one of the most vital contributions to the baby's mental development. It is a skill which should be the first stage of education and can be improved by deliberate daily routine.

As we have noted, the baby's intelligence registers sounds more readily than actual words, although obviously words are the vehicles of the sounds. His name, 'mummy', 'daddy', the names of other siblings, basic objects such as food, drink and so on, can be repeated over and over again when they relate to a person, object, or activity involving the baby. They should be kept simple, without subsidiary words, and not voiced with alternatives – i.e. 'mummy' should not be changed to 'I' or 'me', or the baby's name replaced by 'you'.

Equally important is the tone of the voice, which can convey love just as it can hint at antipathy. Lullabies, which mothers have crooned over their babies since time immemorial, consist largely of meaningless sounds repeated over and over again. The gentle melody and peaceful rhythm are immediately accepted by the baby as reassuring and comforting, whereas a series of words, to the adult mind much more appropriate, will at first convey nothing to the baby until he learns that this stream of sound is a sort of code intended to please him. Far better for him are two or three words spoken clearly but quietly.

The fact that the 'music of words' is the key to a baby's understanding leads to the importance of melody as a vehicle to convey love and to stimulate the burgeoning of memory and intelligence. Everyone can sing after a fashion, and even humming or 'la-la-laing' a tune will delight the youngest baby, particularly if he is being nursed at the time and his mother's face is very close. It has been noted by many child psychologists that babies only a few weeks old move their limbs in an attempt to keep time to a musical rhythm, and their first vocal sounds, other than crying as a result of physical discomfort, are an attempt to imitate the mother's singing sounds.

Melody produced by the human voice, with the singer close enough to the baby for him to see her, is by far the best method of using music in those months before he can understand speech. The use of music through other media needs to be approached with discrimination. Radio, tapes or records blaring away with a vast range and type of sound, almost inevitably much too loud, will at best bewilder the baby as he attempts to absorb some message from it, and at worst jar so much that his defensive mechanism will do its best to shut it out.

Instrumental and recorded vocal tunes have their

place alongside the mother's voice, but the type and duration need to be as carefully chosen as the baby's diet. Solo instruments, with or without a quiet accompaniment, are better than straightforward orchestral pieces. The piece selected should last for a maximum of only five minutes, and during that time the mother should be close to her child, sharing the experience with him. Music is not a robot designed to amuse the baby while his mother gets on with her household chores somewhere else. It cannot be a substitute for her, at least not until daily repetition enables the baby to accept that a familiar stream of sound is the same as the one he heard in the presence of his mother. Even then the session should be brief and the music reproduced very quietly. A baby's sense of hearing is more acute than it will ever be in later life; most adults require a volume of sound which can be alarming to a baby's ears.

That music is a powerful method of developing memory is evident from our own experience. A tune we hear without apparently giving much attention to it will echo and re-echo in our minds. It registers far more easily than, say, a person's name or a telephone number.

Memory is also the means by which knowledge and intelligence are encouraged. In a very young child it can foster his personality and abilities long before he is ready for the routine of conventional education. In short, it gives him a head start.

This is the theory of that remarkable man, Shinichi Suzuki, whose ideas have spread from Japan to every country in the world. The aim of this book is to explain his methods of nurturing a child's potential so as to give full release to his inborn talents. They will help to convince all parents that their child's talents are not an accident of heredity, but his birthright, only waiting for his environment and the help of his parents to release them.

Suzuki does not claim, nor does he wish, to produce a genius. By definition, a human being with extraordinary intellectual power must be the exception. But any normal child can be helped to cultivate all those latent talents with which he was endowed at birth.

The very basis of the Suzuki philosophy is a truth which should have been obvious long ago, but was hardly noticed. It is the phenomenal ability of a young child to learn by listening, well before there is much evidence that he has done so. He observed that children understand what is said to them before they can speak. No matter what language is spoken – even more than one language – they will soon understand the meaning of the words. All the time they are storing this information, and when they begin to speak they can enunciate any language they have learned – coherently and sensibly – far better than an adult with a little experience of a language which is not his or her 'native' one.

No child learns to speak through a course of formal lessons, but by hearing words which are useful to him as they are repeated over and over again, steadily developing his ability to talk by spontaneously repeating the words which impress him, without any insistence from his mother to repeat what she herself has said. Indeed, it is a great mistake to try to encourage her baby to talk by demanding that he repeat a word after her. No young child can be driven to acquire speech at a faster pace than his own needs dictate.

This is one of the important principles of Suzuki teaching. The child is gently led forward by example; never by even the hint of a reward or, in contrast, reproof.

In order to grasp the full significance of this revolutionary approach to the cultivation of human talent, one need do no more than follow the story of the success

Suzuki has achieved during more than forty years of devoted work with children. That he specialises in teaching them to appreciate music and to play music (he regards the violin as the ideal medium) should not disguise the fact that his philosophy is to foster *every* kind of talent. All Suzuki-trained children gain the reward of appreciating music; only a tiny minority will discover that musicianship is the goal for their particular talent. The majority move into adult life as well-developed human beings, assured of the ability to succeed in the field of human knowledge which best suits them.

2 The First Steps

'All children skilfully reared reach a high educational level,' says Suzuki, 'but such rearing must start from the day of birth.'

Note that he does not suggest that a more or less helpless baby should be educated in the formal sense. Critics of the Suzuki philosophy often decry his enthusiasm for a teaching routine long before conventional education begins. He does agree with his friend, Masaru Ibuka, that 'kindergarten is too late', but his beliefs about very early patterns of infant rearing are inspired by his love of children and his desire that those precious early months of life should not be wasted.

Rearing a baby is, in the broad sense, educating a baby. It is so natural and normal that his mother is hardly aware that she is devoting herself to his intellectual and emotional well-being as well as to his physical development. But all three increase at a phenomenal rate in the first months of life and none can develop without the others.

David Lewis, in his book *The Secret Language of Your Child*, writes: 'What can be said with certainty is that bonding between mother and child must take place as soon after the birth as possible, if a good relationship is to be achieved. There is a period of some hours following delivery in which this bonding occurs most easily, strongly and surely. This has been termed the "sensitive period". It is, arguably, the most critical time of our lives.'

Caring for a baby very quickly becomes a matter of routine. It is then that the close bonding of the first contact between mother and new-born child may be unconsciously weakened. The baby is cleansed, washed, fed, and kept warm and comfortable. There may be a temptation to feel that a sleeping baby is a happy and healthy baby.

New-born babies sleep about sixteen hours out of the twenty-four and continue to do so for some three or four months. But that leaves eight hours of wakefulness and, in any event, apart from night-time the periods of sleep are comparatively short. Part of the young baby's waking hours are occupied with feeding and washing and nappy changing, but for at least as long, he is conscious of the small world around him. Those are the times when 'rearing' is so important. The baby should be at least partially upright, nursed against his mother's body and held so that her arms support his back and head. If she sits in an armchair or on a couch, the side can help to support the child and enhance his feeling of security.

It would be an unusual mother who could nurse her baby like this and remain motionless and silent, failing to communicate with him by facial expression. Her gestures of love, inherent in caressing, crooning and smiling, are the key to skilful rearing during the many weeks before language can convey much meaning to the baby.

A young baby receives information from being touched. The gentle pressure of his mother's encircling arms, her stroking of his limbs and head, will evoke responses in his feet and fingers that tell her he finds her caresses comforting. Even more informative to him are his mother's mouth and eyes. Her pursed lips implying a kiss, and above all, her gentle smile, will convey to the child the pleasurable assurance that he is loved and that his mother is happy to be giving him all the attention and affection that she can.

Probably most important of all are the expressions signalled by the eyes, so variable that one cannot easily describe them. Eyes can express friendliness, love and yearning, no matter what their owner may actually say, and they can also hint at boredom, dislike and impatience. By carefully studying a baby's eyes with one's face close to his, it is possible to read his silent reply to one's own eye messages.

Zeno, the ancient Greek philosopher, said, 'Nature has given man one tongue, but two ears that we may hear twice as much as we speak.' He might also have added that Nature has given us two eyes.

Sound and vision are the media through which a young baby learns. He feels no sense of frustration in being incapable of coherent speech. A few simple vocal sounds – gurgling, crying and lip clicking – are all he needs to convey a basic message. For the rest, he depends for his silent language on the movements of his limbs, mouth and eyes.

Sound is pouring information into his brain to a far greater extent than the surroundings visible to him in his restricted environment. He cannot focus on objects some distance from his eyes and therefore ignores them. But he absorbs sounds instantly, and very soon after birth his brain is capable of analysing them; he knows, after experiencing only a few, which are pleasurable or alarming or of little account. What he does dislike, and in time will come to dread, is silence – as if, conscious of his helplessness, he fears he has been deserted.

Constant talking, in a caring and comforting tone of voice, using groups of words that are short and simple, is obviously the major part of this stream of information. 'Mama', 'dada', and some easy version of the baby's own name will be the first words the child learns and, invariably, the first words he speaks. He hears these basic words countless times each day. Repetition aids his memory. It has been noted by researchers that, when he is only about nine weeks old, a baby will react to the small number of words he has been hearing throughout that brief period of his life. He will smile, turn his head, and jerk his arms and legs to indicate pleasure.

In tandem with the silent conversation and the spoken words, Suzuki believes that music can play an equally important role in infant rearing. Melody carries a message for the memory to absorb and retain more easily than the spoken word, and that is why he advocates music as soon as the baby is born.

The mother's voice is not the only suitable source of music, but the quality of any recorded pieces and of their reproduction are important. No child will grow up tone deaf, as it is commonly called, if he has first heard music played at the correct pitch and with a good quality of sound. All the music selected need not be 'classical', although raucous sounds will blunt his sensitivity. Jazz and folk music, as well as some pop, have claims to be heard. As he progresses, your child's own discernment and taste will develop. But do not be surprised if his taste differs radically from year to year.

The music should be played unobtrusively but so that it is just audible. An infant's hearing is so much more sensitive than that of an adult that the sounds he hears must be pleasant to his ears and not alarming or disturbing.

Parents who have enthusiastically adopted the Suzuki philosophy claim that the music should be played three times a day – in the morning, after the baby has been cleansed, fed and has enjoyed his session of cuddling and talking by his mother; then during or after his afternoon feed and, thirdly, as he is put down for his night's sleep.

The final session is the most valuable for fixing the melody in the child's memory. As adults know, one of the best ways of memorising detailed material is to read it last thing at night; it will be strongly implanted, and the student will be word- or figure-perfect the next morning.

There are many examples of the desire of very small children to have this music as a 'tuck-me-up' as they fall asleep. Infants just starting to speak will say 'music' or some invented word if the record player or tape is not switched on as they relax for sleep.

The choice of music rests largely with the parents' taste, assuming that their interest in music ensures that their choice is made from a wide range of musical styles and is acceptable emotionally and intellectually. Remember that you will also be hearing it, several times a day for possibly four or five months, before another piece is chosen to augment the child's musical education. If it was composed by a master and played by a recognised musician it will not pall.

Ideally, it should be a piece by a soloist. Large orchestral pieces can be confusing to a baby's mind, and anyway, they are too long. A recording lasting five minutes or so is quite long enough for this early stage of inculcating appreciation and taste. As the whole concept of the Suzuki system is centred on the violin, it will benefit the future Suzuki student if he hears music played on that instrument rather than on a piano. To give you an idea of suitable pieces, some suggestions are provided at the end of this book.

Encourage your child if he tries to sing with the record. At first his vocal sounds will be isolated and spasmodic. Show your approval by humming the tune yourself now and then. The child will endeavour to imitate both the musical sound and your voice – the first sign that he is being musically educated. No child who imitates tone and pitch in this way will ever be tone-deaf; apart from comparatively rare diseases of the ear, this is not a natural defect but occurs through failure in childhood to learn the gradations of sound in tone and pitch. A child who regularly hears good music, accurately rendered and accurately reproduced, will recreate those accurate sounds with his own voice.

It may surprise you to realise that at three months your baby is capable of producing every vocal sound he will ever need to speak and sing. While he is awake he is hungry for information conveyed by sound, whether it originates in speech, music or the general sounds of his environment. Jean Piaget, a Swiss psychologist who devoted his life to the study of children, has written, 'The more a child has seen and heard the more he wants to see and hear.'

In some parts of the world, notably in the USA, recognition of a young child's eagerness to learn has resulted in reading being taught to children as soon as they can speak. Every day, cards carrying an illustration plus the relevant word, such as a picture of a cat with the word 'cat' printed below it, are placed in front of the child while the word is spoken. In a remarkably short time, cards bearing only the word and no illustration are substituted, and more often than not, the child will say the word correctly. His brain has registered the word as a coded pattern symbolising the picture which originally accompanied the pattern. We all learn some code-signs in this way: that a numeral, based on Arabic script, in fact stands for a word; '8' is a shorthand method of writing 'eight'; '&' stands for the three-letter word 'and'; '£' must be spoken as if it were spelled out as 'pound'.

The child learning to 'read' by the picture-and-name system will later have to learn that the pattern he could recognise as a word in fact consists of separate letters, each with its own sound. Until then, the word on the picture he sees might as well have been in Egyptian hieroglyphics or a foreign language.

It is small wonder that this pressure on a young child to recognise simple combinations of letters, such as cat, dog, doll, and so on, may ultimately cause him to become fractious and restless, displaying signs of stress as he is encouraged to solve what to him is a puzzle. The Suzuki philosophy is the antithesis of this, using music as a method of leading the child to steady and natural development of his intelligence and memory. Music, in Suzuki's view, presents the child with a form of pleasurable interest rather than a difficult activity where mistakes are all too easy to make.

Parents who adopt this music listening programme invariably ask, 'how long?' A short and rather unsatisfactory answer would be, 'for as long as it is enjoyable to the child.' If it begins shortly after birth, when the child will be unable to voice his own feelings for a couple of years, this is clearly an inordinately long period to play the same piece possibly three times a day. What is certain is that the presence of music to listen to must remain part of daily living. With the exception of bedtime, when the child is virtually certain to want to be soothed to sleep with the familiar and well-loved tune, times of playing can be varied. Mealtimes are ideal; so is playtime, with the child amusing himself with toys or just crawling or toddling around the room. So long as his mother is present and is apparently sharing the experience, there will be no risk that he might see the music as a substitute for her loving presence.

No parent plans speaking lessons, privately yearning for the day when the child is word perfect. No parent reports that he or she spent hours and hours asking a child to repeat words, eventually admitting that she had abandoned the lessons as the child appeared to have no aptitude for, or interest in, talking. Teaching a child to talk goes on automatically every day. It can be the same with music. The possibilities of appreciating it more and more are endless.

To persist may well require patience. Just as small children demand to be told the same nursery rhyme or fairy tale time after time, with every word the same as before, so they will continue to enjoy the piece of music first selected for their education and entertainment, long after an adult may be bored almost to distraction.

But some new pieces can gradually be chosen for contrast and variety. A vocal piece, choral music, other solo instruments such as the piano, 'cello, or flute, can be added. These will develop the child's ability to discriminate, and he will voice his preference, asking for the new piece until he has become thoroughly familiar with it, before he selects yet another as the current favourite. The earlier and more familiar pieces should not be abandoned. The child will gain great pleasure from hearing again the piece he knows so well.

Any parent who is able to play a musical instrument can test the acute hearing of her child by regularly playing a favourite piece and then one day inserting a wrong note. The child will instantly notice it.

The use of music as a method of fostering talent needs to be adopted with sensible moderation. In many homes the radio or transistor is switched on for hour after hour, the music just a drug-like background to the daily routine. This 'wallpaper music' will not only spoil a child's musical taste, but his defence mechanism will attempt to ignore it, along with other extraneous sounds which are unimportant to him.

By the age of two years the musically educated child will be ready to enjoy the treat of hearing a concert, or at least part of one. There are plenty of good concerts on the BBC Radio Three and Radio Four programmes and occasionally on BBC2 TV. Listening to them deserves to be made into an occasion, shared with the whole family giving the music their full attention. No one, having paid to hear a live concert as a member of the audience, would read a newspaper or chatter during the performance. The same degree of uninterrupted attention is justified when the concert is heard at home, and the most active child will sit listening happily on his mother's or father's lap if he can see that his family is paying close attention to the music and that he is privileged to do the same.

The programme should be selected with some care, with a piece which lasts no longer than about twenty minutes. That is probably the maximum a small child can really absorb in one session. He should not be forced to go on listening to the entire concert or to a long symphony with several movements, for then something that began as a treat will be in danger of becoming a perplexing task.

Video tapes have introduced an additional and invaluable tool for this home education in music. Not only will the child's interest be increased by watching as well as listening, but he will learn how an instrument creates the sounds he has been hearing. His ability to imitate will extend to the first stages of recognising how an instrument is held and why its strings can be made to produce varying notes.

Careful visual study by parents will also prove useful in subsequent years. Statistics indicate that only a small minority of parents has ever learned even the rudimentary techniques of violin playing, and that not many can play the piano. This lack is no obstacle to the adoption of Suzuki Talent Education methods; it can even be an advantage because the gap inherent in the teacher-pupil role does not exist.

Suzuki stresses that the parent should be a fellow-pupil, and the principle at the very centre of Suzuki's teaching is that in early musical training the family is the most resourceful unit in encouraging a small child's interest. His mother is accepted, as in every other aspect of instruction, as the senior pupil, but still a pupil, and if she is obviously excited and interested, then the child will copy her.

The mother will, of course, know the title of the piece of music the child likes, but before the age of two the child should also be able to identify it by name. If the title is difficult to pronounce a 'pet name' can be invented. The mother should say the name of the piece both before and after playing it, and as soon as the child has learned it he should be encouraged to say it. By asking him, 'Which tape would you like to hear first?' and then, 'Let's see, what was the name of the piece we've been enjoying?' he will come to understand that every piece of music has a title. This growth of awareness can be extended by mentioning the name of the composer and later of the performer.

Most record sleeves and cassettes have illustrations of the performer and can be readily identified by a child of two years. He can then be asked to pick out the record or tape he and his mother have decided to hear.

The more active a child's participation in the listening sessions, the more eagerness he will display for them. Occasions which may occur, when he says he doesn't want to listen or starts to play a noisy game, indicate frustration at his passive role rather than boredom.

Let him share the simple preparation, not only by identifying the record or cassette, but by switching on the player and placing the record or tape in position. Below the age of three, moving the pick-up arm onto a record (in the case of non-automatic players) may be tricky, but a cassette can be easily inserted, and the 'play' button and volume control will present no problem. The tone control is best left at the position midway between bass and treble, to ensure that the reproduction is faithful to the recording.

Gradually the repertoire should be increased to at least half a dozen pieces, but not all should be played during one session, as this would mean around an hour of listening. Let the child share in the choice each time, encouraging him to choose a new piece in addition to his favourite and familiar one. 'Shall we play that new Mozart minuet?' – 'I'd like to hear that piano concerto, wouldn't you?' are the kinds of suggestion which will enable to child to agree or disagree. If his reaction is to select something else, accept it, but repeat your suggestion the next day.

When does Suzuki believe it is time for a child to begin to learn to play? The general practice is at the age of three, by which time the average child will be sufficiently physically developed to enable him to hold a violin and bow properly. If listening to music began shortly after birth, there will by then have been around three thousand sessions, on the basis of an average of three per day. That is a formidable total. It may well have necessitated replacing worn-out records or cassettes, and it is naturally a daunting prospect for even the most devoted of parents.

It must be said that some start with enthusiasm only to abandon the idea, because it seems such a long time before the desired goal will be achieved of rearing a child who can play a violin. It is all too tempting to slacken off; holidays, times of ill-health, the changes in the general routine of bringing up a fast-growing child, can all cause interruptions so that the listening routine is modified or delayed for long intervals. This is a pity, for all the early preparation is then largely wasted, and when the child reaches the age when he can start to play he is bereft of advantages he will regain only with some difficulty.

'Parents often let the precious days go by,' says

Suzuki. 'They try to educate their children when it is too late. Finally they give up with the excuse, "Well, it seems my child was born without talent". These parents fully deserve to be called careless, for they have let the youngster's only chance slip by. Yet they talk of talent as though it could not be developed by careful upbringing.'

Suzuki clearly does not mince his words in stressing his confident assertion that the foundations of talent must start in early babyhood. But there is no need for parents to feel a sense of failure or carelessness, simply because they had never even heard of Suzuki's ideas until their child was a year or eighteen months old. Fortunately, such is a small child's ability to absorb information that starting a little late can be just as beneficial. The great objective should be to attain something like the standards outlined in the previous pages.

The age of three, then, or very soon afterwards, marks the time when music should cease to be only a passive activity. A more active participation can now begin.

It is a time of decision for the parents. Hitherto Talent Education has been entirely a family activity. Now professional help and advice is needed – and for both child and mother.

It must be stressed that the mother cannot retire gracefully into the role of part-time adviser and theorist. She will be expected to join in, either by learning with her child to play the violin or by making herself conversant with the techniques through paying careful attention during lessons and asking the teacher about anything which is unclear to her. Do not be put off by the thought of some kind of active participation, even if you do not wish to go so far as actually learning the violin yourself. The thrill of working with your child will provide an impetus which will carry you through.

There will also be some expense involved for musical instruments and teacher's fees. Whether this modest investment in the child's future, not to mention the adult's satisfaction in taking part in the learning process, is worthwhile, is for the parents to decide. It would be a pity to abandon the devotion of those first years, just as its success is about to become obvious.

3 The Man from Matsumoto

One of Shinichi Suzuki's favourite stories concerns a parakeet, the pet of two small children he knew. The bird was able to say its name, Peeko, and a number of sentences, using the high-pitched tones of the children. Nothing unusual in that, of course, but Suzuki was fascinated by the evidence that a bird, well known to be able to imitate sounds, could, without natural or inherited ability, adopt the sounds of human language.

He was told by the children's parents that the bird had been bought as a pet when still a fledgling. Its name of Peeko was voiced on an average fifty times a day for two months – a total of three thousand repetitions. The bird then 'spoke' his name as a greeting whenever he was approached by the children.

Suzuki realised that without this assiduous coaching the bird would never have appeared clever or unusual. The desired result was only achieved in two months through the stimulus of preparation, time and environment.

No one, and certainly not Suzuki, would expect a child of only a few months to be subjected to the monotonous and meaningless repetition of a single word – the baby's name, for instance – fifty times a day for two months. In practice, of course, a small number of words are quite naturally repeated over and over again during a mother's routine daily care of her child, and will easily reach a total of several thousand in a period of two or three months.

At first, there is no evidence that the child, although reacting with pleasure to his mother's voice, is preparing to speak himself. As Suzuki puts it, the beginning is slow until the 'bud of ability' takes hold. At first it will develop slowly, but ability breeds more ability, and the period needed for the first word or two decreases until learning to speak a whole range of words becomes spontaneous. By the age of two years a normal child will have a vocabulary of some two hundred words – entirely learned by listening to and imitating his parents. At the age of four he will be able to speak at least 1,500 words – again, only if he has heard them.

Suzuki adopted this evidence of a young child's ability to learn to speak as the secret of expanding his intellect through music, a medium which knows no boundaries through language differences, and which develops intellect, emotions and physique. The prominence he gives to the violin as a means of fostering a child's talent results from his own love of the instrument, but the basis of his teaching applies to any musical instrument, and indirectly to all skills and intellectual activities.

Suzuki was born in Matsumoto, a city in the mountainous area of Western Japan. He was inevitably attracted to music because his family owned a violin factory, producing large number of high quality violins every year, as it still does. Despite these family traditions, young Suzuki was given no tuition in violin playing. Enthralled by listening to a gramophone record of Schubert's *Ave Maria* played by Mischa Elman, at the time regarded as one of the world's great violinists, he brought home a violin from that day's output and tried to accompany the recording.

Day after day he practised. He had no score and there was no one to teach him. At first his efforts were inevitably little more than discordant scrapings, but occasionally he produced tones he had never realised were possible. With persistence he was able eventually to play a recognisable version of *Ave Maria* and of another piece on a second record, a minuet by Haydn. He has since admitted that he never became more than a passable violinist because self-tuition produced too many bad habits which became so strongly established that it was not possible completely to eradicate them.

This statement deserves to be borne in mind by any parent who fails to appreciate the true basis of Suzuki's methods of teaching. It is not a do-it-yourself system in which parents with little or no ability to play the violin, or any other instrument, can successfully teach a child by a home-made version of the Suzuki programme of lessons. The almost inevitable result will be disappointment for the child and exasperation for his untrained teachers. An amateur imitation of a rendering on tape or record is not enough. There must be professional guidance.

That does not mean that the parent should step aside. On the contrary, active co-operation is essential. Any parent who believes he or she has not the time or interest to progress step by step with the child will also have to accept that there is little chance of the child really benefiting from the Suzuki philosophy.

Through force of circumstances, Suzuki was not fortunate enough to enjoy the professional help he needed until he was twenty years old. Only then was he able to persuade his father to allow him to go to Germany and study under accomplished European teachers. He knew virtually nothing about life in the Western world and was unaware that Germany was still striving to repair the economic ruin which followed the First World War.

He arrived in Berlin, hoping to get by on the

smattering of English he had been taught at school but with no knowledge of the German language. With German inflation out of control and the Deutschmark almost worthless, the modest sum in Japanese money Suzuki had brought with him easily enabled him to obtain lodgings in Berlin. For days he just roamed about the city, reading advertisement posters and street signs in order to learn a few words of German. He listened to conversations in cafés and among his fellow lodgers, slowly gaining a few words he could understand and pronounce with difficulty.

The language problem triggered thoughts which, if he had fully realised it, gave him the seeds of his idea for a new system of education for very young children. It was the sight of children playing in the courtyard outside his lodgings. They chattered to one another in what seemed to him to be fluent German, easily stringing words into sentences, whereas he could speak to them only haltingly, and could understand only a word here and there when they spoke to him.

'Little German children spoke and understood German. Japanese children can all speak Japanese. The thought suddenly struck me with amazement. In fact, all children throughout the world speak their native tongues with the utmost fluency . . . It made me realise that any child is able to display highly superior abilities if only the correct methods are used in training.'

Suzuki pondered on this universal ability of two and three year-olds to understand and speak their mother tongue. It was clearly not a natural inheritance. It must be through training by a perfect educational method. And that method did not involve classes, tests, punishments or rewards, but a ceaseless daily routine of parents, relatives and visitors just talking. The child, still an infant and regarded as two or three years away from the need for any scholastic education, listened, memorised and imitated. Educating the child in his mother tongue was automatic and unavoidable, so that in a far shorter period than would be possible for him in later life he became capable of using intelligent speech as a means of communication.

At the time of Suzuki's sudden fascination with the phenomenal rate of language learning among children who otherwise displayed no special talent, he evidently did not fully realise that tone, rhythm and expression in the words they heard were ingredients of the knowledge they absorbed. These resulted in the children speaking with the same accents and vowel sounds as those of their 'teachers'; hence they not only spoke intelligible words but they imitated the dialect and the sing-song tones which embellish human speech, in contrast to the soulless precision of words reproduced mechanically – as in today's electronically created speech of so-called talking robots.

Suzuki then came to accept the power of music to communicate – a form of language universally understood. He had sought out the best teacher he could find in Berlin, Karl Klingler. He had gone to a recital given by the violinist's quartet and was so enthralled by the performance that he painfully composed a letter in English, ending with the request, 'please take me as your pupil'.

Although Klinger was reputed not to take pupils for individual private tuition, he sent Suzuki a one-word message: 'Come'. He went to Klingler's home the next day. Conversation between the two was virtually impossible; at first they relied on music, Klingler playing a short piece and Suzuki attempting to imitate it. The lessons developed into several sessions a week, with Suzuki improving his playing and, more slowly, picking up the meaning of his teacher's advice in German.

Klingler introduced Suzuki to a wide circle of musicians

and music lovers. One of them was Max Bruch, a composer well known for his works for the violin and 'cello. As Bruch had for a time lived in England, as conductor of the Liverpool Philharmonic Orchestra, he was able to speak English with Suzuki and help him overcome the language barrier.

Through Bruch, Suzuki met Albert Einstein who regularly held musical evenings at his home. The scientist, already famous for his theories on relativity, was a skilled performer on the violin, and indeed throughout his long life played the instrument for his own pleasure and relaxation.

Einstein's stories about his childhood gave Suzuki yet more food for thought on the value of music to fertilise still-dormant talent. Einstein told how, as a small child, he had been shy, timid and slow to speak. Some of his relations barely concealed their suspicion that the child was mentally subnormal. His parents, however, had noticed how, from early infancy, he had reacted with obvious pleasure to music. They bought him a small violin. Before he was six years old he was having lessons from a professional teacher.

Asked how he had first come to ponder on the problem which eventually yielded his theory of relativity, Einstein told his guests, 'It occurred to me by intuition, and music was the driving force behind that intuition. My discovery was the result of musical perception.'

Suzuki was deeply impressed by Einstein's words. If knowledge of music could release the powers of intuition, then music could be the key to fostering talent in anyone. He did not expect that it would produce a genius of the Einstein standard, but it seemed feasible that it would foster talent in children which would otherwise remain latent.

For eight years Suzuki remained in Berlin, devoting all his time to music. On his return to Japan he began to try out his ideas of early introduction to playing music among a steadily increasing number of children. His reputation grew, entirely through the comments of delighted parents to their friends.

The prolonged period of war in China, and then against the Western Allies, inevitably affected the Suzuki programme of Talent Education. The family factory was allocated war work and the manufacture of violins virtually ceased. Suzuki, who loathed the very idea of war, managed to maintain a token version of his teaching, but not until 1947 was he able to found his Talent Education Institute.

At first many people – educationalists and parents alike – believed that the Institute was aiming to give small children a flying start in education so that it would produce, if not prodigies, then at least highly trained youngsters destined to be tomorrow's political leaders, inventors, industrial tycoons – the elite of society destined for certain success after the full course of training.

A few meetings with Suzuki altered this view. He explained that every child attending his Institute was given the chance to develop talents already in existence but dormant until brought into activity by 'total human education', resulting in the development of general knowledge, moral precepts, and a strong character. Playing and appreciating music he regarded as a form of release of a child's potential.

The success of the Talent Education Institute spread steadily throughout Japan and then to other countries. TV programmes in Europe and the USA, showing very small children playing violins with impressive ability, aroused the interest of parents and teachers. Groups of enthusiasts were formed, so that Suzuki was obliged to provide instructional books in English.

Many people involved in the education of children

found it difficult to agree with the Suzuki claim that 'all children skilfully reared reach a high educational standard but such rearing must start from the day of birth'. No professional teachers, they pointed out, were involved with new-born babies. Parents normally did not consider educational matters until their children were walking and talking, and usually not until they were old enough to go to pre-school groups. The idea seemed to go against the conventional patterns of child education, with their accent on literacy as the first step. The only modern development had been in encouraging small children to develop a visual talent with free expression through painting and drawing. Suzuki, however, believed that music was the most effective way of releasing intelligence, its influence being obvious at a very early age.

He has recounted the story of a five month-old baby. The child was brought in her mother's arms to a class where the baby's six year-old sister was a pupil in a Suzuki class. The older girl had been learning to play a concerto by Vivaldi and had been listening to a recording of the piece every day at home.

Suzuki wanted to know what effect this constant repetition had had on the baby who was usually in the room when the record was played. He watched the baby's face while he played a Bach minuet on the violin. The baby's eyes moved to locate the source of the music which she was hearing for the first time. The reaction was no more than a slight interest. Suzuki then played the Vivaldi piece which the older girl had played day after day. The baby's facial expression immediately changed. She smiled, turned to gaze into her mother's face and began moving her arms and legs in rhythm to the music. It was obvious that she recognised the melody—it was *her* music.

The importance of fostering an interest in good music

from babyhood is therefore stressed as the first step towards the Suzuki method of talent education. Obviously, his practical lessons in violin playing cannot start until the child has grown enough to hold a violin and bow, but because the principle of his theory on bringing talent to full fruition includes education from babyhood, it is never too early for parents to make a start.

Many thousands of children have in the past forty years benefited from Suzuki teaching, and time has now proved that it does indeed produce, not necessarily musicians of great talent, but adults who are talented in whatever field of human activity they choose.

4 Parents are Both Pupils and Teachers

If you have been using music as an integral part of rearing your child from babyhood to the age of three, there should be no problem about his desire to be more than a passive listener.

The other members of the family, however, may have some objections which need to be faced and dealt with. What are the reactions among your child's brothers and sisters, older or younger? Will the time and attention you will be giving daily to the new Suzuki trainee arouse jealousy among any older children because they have missed what seems to them to be preferential treatment? Can you cope with this kind of special caring for any new baby brother or sister as well?

Then there is the opinion of the father. Generally speaking, Suzuki prefers that one parent, usually the mother, is the home supervisor of Suzuki education, with the other partner restricting his contribution to encouragement and tolerance. The best of husbands can present occasional problems.

I have been told of the head of the family coming home, tired after a day's work, unable to hide his exasperation that the same very familiar tune is being played yet again, while he receives a whispered order to keep quiet. Perhaps his evening meal is delayed or he cannot switch on the TV news. If he actually complains, or if he shows he is annoyed by going to some other room for peace and quiet, there will be family tension, not least for the child who will be conscious that somehow a happy time has been ruined and who may feel that it is his fault.

For the mother there will be personal problems. If she has a job, it will be an almost insuperable difficulty to work out an ideal home and workplace routine. For any mother, some outside social activities will have to be adjusted or dropped. When the time comes for classes it will not simply be a matter of seeing that the child gets there and back safely, as in the case of Cubs and Brownies or play-school.

It is important to assess the demands which will be made on your time and see how sensible adjustments can be made in your daily routine. Given a genuine desire to continue with the good work already undertaken, and realising how much your child has already developed in character and intellect, you will most likely feel that your child's welfare is all-important.

A final, mundane factor needs to be considered. Suzuki education, even if you are fortunate enough to live in an area where much of the tuition is available under the State education system, is not cheap. A violin must be purchased (and ideally a second one for yourself); there will be Suzuki Books to buy; at least part of the early tuition, when not more than four pupils are taught in one hour, will involve the payment of fees.

Later, when we discuss musical instruments, you will learn some idea of the cost, and in subsequent pages the general rates of teaching fees will be covered. You will then see that the price of this investment in your child's future is a good one, although quite high.

The mother of seven year-old Karen told me that she and her husband had had misgivings when they considered Suzuki training nearly four years before. Then they got things in perspective.

'I attend a weekly keep-fit class right through the winter months,' she said. 'My husband is a soccer fan and follows his team to most away games, as well as those on the home ground. We rent a video as well as a TV and we run a car. Totting up what we both spend on these things proved that giving Karen a real chance in life was a minor sum. She's doing well in all her subjects at school as well as in her Suzuki class. I reckon her educational standards are higher than she would have attained at the most expensive private school and at about a tenth of the cost. I think that the suspicion that we would have to buy several violins of increased sizes put us off. But we found that we could part-exchange the smaller violin for a larger one, and once we were allowed more than we had paid for it the year before.'

Once tuition begins, you will become involved in a regular routine. First of all, the teacher will want to give you yourself a course of tuition, probably with weekly lessons for a couple of months. This will give you a basic knowledge of the technique and you will be able to hold violin and bow properly, and produce a recognisable melody.

When your child attends lessons, usually once a week, you will have to be present. Later there may be additional lessons with small groups of pupils.

At home there will be daily practice. At first each session can be as brief as five minutes, repeated after a break for playtime, meals, outings to the shops and so on. You will practise with the child.

Listening to music should continue in the familiar routine, and you will probably have a tape or record of the piece being taught – *Twinkle, twinkle, little star*. Not only is this a tune which the youngest child enjoys for its melody and simplicity, but it is playable in all sorts of variations.

Practice at home is almost as important as the lessons.

It needs discipline from the mother who doubtless has many chores she needs to fit into the daily round. The average child, already 'sold' on the attractions of music, will not be awkward or obstinate when practice time comes round. He enjoys this development too much. If he does occasionally complain that he knows it all and would rather do something else, tell him Suzuki's humorous advice: 'You don't have to practise on the days you don't eat!'

And that advice about daily practice applies also to yourself. Every child wants to imitate his parent – boys copying their fathers, girls their mothers, plus a degree of imitation across the sex difference, so that mannerisms, speech pronunciation and habits are copied from both parents. No teacher has ever heard of a child who was not impatient to attempt to play if the mother started practising first. From the earliest days, practising can be encouraged by a policy of 'do as I do', not 'do as I say'. No child should be forced to practise. Threats such as 'if you don't practise, there'll be no TV for you this evening', and rewards on the lines of 'do your practice and you can have an ice cream' will not achieve the desired progress. What can and should be a pleasure becomes a dreaded duty.

No parent should seriously adopt Suzuki's ideas unless she has been impressed by them, and usually excited as well. The fact that very young children are seen playing in groups to a high standard tempts the newly enrolled parent to expect rapid results. They are indeed rapid compared with the progress by conventional teaching. A pupil who goes through the complete Suzuki course will, by the age of twelve or thirteen, be some four years ahead of a youngster who did not start to learn to play until he began his schooling.

But this optimism in the efficiency of the Suzuki methods can make parents impatient to see results far sooner than is justified. No one gets annoyed because an infant prefers to crawl rather than walk when other children of the same age are toddling about; nor does any loving parent feel despair because her child seems very slow to increase the number of spoken words in his vocabulary. Lessons in walking are gentle and brief; there aren't x numbers of new words to learn and speak every day.

It is the same with the first weeks of playing a violin – demanding an effort far greater than that involved in walking and talking. Patience must be the policy, for at first there will be only slight evidence of progress. But the child will be storing knowledge and preparing to use it as soon as he has overcome all the difficulties of co-ordination between mind and muscle, making arm and hand movements which have not been previously needed, and analysing the individual sounds which combine to produce the music he loves to hear.

Children's mental and physical development does vary, and there can be no hard and fast rule about the precise time that learning to play should begin. Some children are certainly mature enough at three to start, and a few, as Suzuki has discovered, are ready several weeks before their third birthday. Many more are not ready until they are four or five, the latter age usually being regarded as the latest if the full benefit of the Suzuki philosophy is to be enjoyed.

To a great extent, the starting time for planned tuition will depend on the teacher. The majority find that a short time before the fifth birthday is best both from their point of view and that of the parents. If you do find a teacher who is enthusiastic about starting as soon as possible after the third birthday, you are fortunate; she has emulated the ideals laid down by Suzuki and is thoroughly convinced that they work.

Every Suzuki-trained teacher stresses the part the

parent has the play. She herself is the professional, but she wants the child's parent to be her partner, senior pupil, and adviser. Neither can succeed without the other. Even though the child is now learning to play an instrument, his continuing education in other areas of music – essential if he is to accept that the violin or other instrument is just part of a wide world of music – is still in the hands of his parents. What has been said in Chapter Two is still relevant, but it will be necessary to help him to explore this world of music even further, in line with his own musical development and any aspects which emerge during his music lessons.

Radio and TV sets, records and cassettes can provide an inexhaustible source of music which a child will enjoy and which will enhance his knowledge. Select a transmitted musical programme with discrimination and make it a family concert you watch and listen to, rather than a background to other activities. Both BBC and ITV programme weeklies include some details of the items in a concert and of the composers and players. Use this information before the programme begins to increase the child's interest. All record sleeves and cassettes provide fuller details, with anecdotes about the composer and artistes which will intrigue the child and give the human touch so easily forgotten in listening to recorded music.

A young child is likely to become restless after half an hour's programme of music. This is approximately the duration of most LPs and cassettes. In the case of radio and TV concerts, you can select just one piece from the programme. Symphonies are not really suitable; they are too long and the themes and treatment are involved. The best items are by soloists, either playing an instrument, perhaps with an orchestral accompaniment, or singing. In the latter case be sure the words are in English.

The cost of cassettes and records is not really very great, considering that they can provide years of pleasure. They have the advantage that they give your child the opportunity to help choose them. He will enjoy a visit to a record shop, looking at the illustrations on the covers, and trying out one or two in a listening booth. The purchase can be a gift for him – tangible proof that he can have his own piece of music buried in a disc or tiny box.

There need not be even this modest expense every time you want some new music. Most larger public libraries loan records and cassettes which can be used for two or three weeks. If your child falls in love with one of these borrowed pieces you can then buy him the same recording at the record shop.

The question of taste will sometimes arise. You may choose to listen to or buy a piece of music that you know you will enjoy and that you expect your child to like, too. If he is unimpressed or says outright that he does not like it, don't imply that he isn't clever enough to appreciate how good it is, but let him know that you personally think you are getting to like it.

Tacitly he always respects your opinion and, even if he really does not agree with you, he will ponder on the fact that you like it and may indeed come round to your way of thinking after he has heard the tune a few times. If he continues to grumble, accept that tastes differ; just because he is very young it does not mean he is wrong. Tolerance and respect for the child's point of view are vital. If you hint that you are right and he is silly, and that you know best, he will nurse his own form of bigotry and be as determined to stick to his own opinion as you are.

As you increase the variety of music to which you both listen, he should be given the chance to absorb contrasting ideas in the 'message' of music, and to discover the different moods and rhythms. Initially it may seem that he is most impressed by loud and dramatic music. But there will also be times when he will prefer a quiet solo, either vocal or instrumental. All children like lullaby tunes, for example.

You may well be able to pick out a variety of kinds of music from your own experience, or else from the title of a piece. Otherwise, you can seek expert advice. Public libraries which lend recordings often maintain lists of music suitable for children, although they will frequently be of the novelty type with little musical quality. The better type of record and music shop will have a music lover on the staff who will suggest suitable recordings for young children, particularly if you explain that you plan for your child to have music lessons in the near future. Alternatively, you can consult the selection of pieces for children in this older age group given at the end of this book.

A word should be said here about so-called programme music, or background music, directly related to a play, story, or well known programme. TV, radio and film producers spend much time and thought on the theme music intended to enhance the emotional impact of a plot. Other tunes have little to do with the story but become familiar through constant repetition so that the music becomes a signpost to the programme that follows. Most people can identify a tune preceding the programme which follows this signature tune, as in popular serials like *The Archers* and *Coronation Street*. But the music bears little relation to the story line.

Music does not usually reflect the factual material of a story. It is more concerned with mood and appeals to the emotions. There are, of course, great works which do succeed in depicting the scenes embodied in the title. Beethoven's *Pastoral* Symphony and Vivaldi's *The Four Seasons* are examples. By all means tell your child beforehand that this kind of music will paint a picture in sound, but remember that he does not need too much explanation, as that would restrict his own imagination in feeling spontaneously what the music means.

Do not isolate your child from hearing pop, jazz and folk music. Some of it is rubbish, but many pieces have stood the test of time and have quality. Equally, if a piece of music is placed in the 'classical' category, it does not mean that it automatically has a claim to be 'worthwhile'. Much pretentious rubbish appears in this category also. Listening to a wide variety of music will help the child to weigh one style against another and so develop a discriminatory sense.

The more music a child hears the more interested he will become in the instruments which produce it. Apart from watching performances on TV and radio, he will enjoy the treat of being taken to live performances. Excellent children's concerts are presented in the larger towns at Christmas time, and there are many summer tours by famous orchestras which reach town halls and theatres in scores of cities. Choose an afternoon performance and check that the programme includes pieces a small child can enjoy.

Prokofiev's *Peter and the Wolf* will both delight him and teach him about the part each instrument plays in creating the music. Each character in the fable is represented by a single instrument or group of instruments. As the music begins a narrator explains which instrument will identify which character, and thereafter an occasional comment recounts the development of the story.

Benjamin Britten's *The Young Person's Guide to the Orchestra* is a more complex work with a mass of information which a young child may find difficult to appreciate at first. However, it is a unique source of knowledge which a child as young as four or five can absorb if he can see and hear it several times. Ideally it should be in a video or home movie version, but the recording will, after being played regularly and repeatedly, enable the child to identify an instrument by its sound.

Britten took a theme by Henry Purcell which is first played a number of times by the full orchestra or by sections of it, in order to implant the melody in the young listener's mind. Then follows a variation for each instrument, bringing them all back together with a fugue (the composition in which a melodic theme is introduced by one instrument and is taken up by the others). The description sounds complicated but the music becomes simple when heard often and is then quite easily understood by a child. If you obtain the recording there will be a folder with full explanatory notes to be read aloud while the music is being played.

At some stage during your home education programme you will be bound to ask yourself if all the time and trouble is producing results. The simple answer is that success cannot be tabulated in any mundane way. You have been steadily sowing the seeds of musical knowledge and they will take time to germinate. Yet you can be certain that those seeds are no longer dormant but are being nourished.

'Children are like seeds planted in the ground,' says Suzuki. 'They must be watered daily. With constant care and attention the seed will grow into a plant and eventually flower.' Given that daily care and attention, there will in time be definite signs of development. The child who looks forward to the musical session and does not protest that he would rather do something else is clearly regarding listening to music as a treat and not a duty.

'I didn't believe he was really listening,' Alistair's mother told me after almost two years of this daily listening programme. 'Before he was three he was content to sit on my lap and listen quietly. Then he started to toddle around the room and play with his toys. But one day, when he was out in the garden, I heard him humming snatches of a tune. It was the one we had played earlier that morning. After that I sometimes made a poor attempt to "la-la-la" the melody. He began to join in. Then I knew that he really had been absorbing the tune even though I didn't think he was taking much notice.'

Since that time Alistair has joined a Suzuki class. His mother had a few piano lessons as a child until she found them boring and gave up. The basic knowledge about notes made it simpler for her to work with Alistair's teacher to learn to play the violin. On the advice of the teacher and Alistair's own preference, after he had seen a TV programme of small Japanese violin players, he also opted for the violin. That made it easier to find a Suzuki-trained teacher. Most follow Suzuki's policy of making the violin the standard instrument in his Talent Education programme.

But the principles of the system can apply to other instruments, notably the 'cello and piano. Many parents have ambitions for their child to be taught some instrument other than the violin. Before a decision is made it will be worth while considering the pros and cons of the instruments which a boy or girl may successfully handle and learn to play.

5   The Music Makers

It is a virtual certainty that your local Suzuki teacher will
be primarily interested in violin tuition. Suzuki believes
it to be the ideal instrument on which to introduce a
young child to the playing of music, and the most
promising for achieving a skilled performance. Neither
he nor any devoted follower of his ideas insists that the
Suzuki teaching methods exclude other instruments,
and many pupils have been taught piano playing by
much the same method. Once the ability to play music
has been inculcated by the routine of learning the violin,
changing to some other instrument becomes much less
difficult.

A child who has seen and heard an orchestral
performance is well aware that all musical instruments
are interesting. He may tell himself that one day he will
learn to play one that particularly enthralled him. The
desire may lie dormant while he is still young, either to
fade once he achieves some skill on the violin or to
survive years later when he is able to make an intelligent
choice.

In any event, it will foster his general interest in music
if he can readily identify an instrument by sound, sight
or both. His parents will also appreciate a performance if
they learn along with him, turning the session of
listening to a concert into a quiz, with occasional
questions such as, 'Was that a flute?' 'What is that large

stringed instrument on the right of the picture?' so long as the questions do not detract from enjoyment of the music.

Here, in alphabetical order, are the principal solo and orchestral instruments. The list is followed by some information on those instruments which may be taught to children by some modification of the Suzuki system for violin tuition.

Bassoon   The woodwind instrument with the lowest tone. It has a double reed.

Bugle   A brass instrument with a conical tube and cup-shaped mouthpiece. It is played almost exclusively as an instrument in military activities or by juveniles in Boy Scouts' and Boys' Brigade bands.

'Cello   Its full name is violoncello. A stringed instrument with a bass range. It is supported between the knees of a sitting player and by a spike on the floor. In some jazz and pop groups it is played with the instrumentalist standing. It is a member of the violin family.

Clarinet   A woodwind instrument with a single reed. It was greatly liked by Mozart who was responsible for it gaining an established place in an orchestra.

Cornet   A brass instrument similar to the trumpet but with a rounder tone, used mainly in brass bands.

Double bass   The largest and deepest-sounding of the violin family of instruments, usually played standing, or seated on a high stool.

English horn (Cor anglais)   A woodwind instrument with a double reed. It is in the oboe family and has a lower range than the normal oboe.

Flute   A woodwind instrument played while held side-ways. There is no reed. It is available in several sizes. The sound is made by blowing across a hole in the tube.

French horn   A brass instrument with a coiled tube of conical bore ending in a bell shape. There can be from two to eight of them in a symphony orchestra. The name is derived from the French hunting horn. The modern instrument is highly sophisticated and can be very heavy to hold.

Guitar   A stringed instrument which is plucked or strummed, not played with a bow.

Horn   The usual abbreviated name for the French horn.

Lute   A stringed instrument plucked with the fingers. It is now played mainly in concerts of early musical compositions.

Mandolin   An instrument with paired strings played with a plectrum held in the hand, today rarely used except as a solo instrument.

Oboe   A woodwind instrument with a double reed. It is an important instrument both in an orchestra or for solo performances.

Pianoforte   A keyboard instrument in which the strings are struck by felt-covered hammers. It ranks with the violin among the important solo instruments.

Recorder   A woodwind instrument which was the forerunner of the flute. The group includes soprano, descant, treble, tenor and bass versions. Because of its comparative simplicity it is now popular for basic music teaching to small children.

Saxophone   A brass wind instrument with a single reed made in various pitches from soprano to bass. It has many affinities with the clarinet.

Timpani   There are usually at least two or three in an orchestra, all played by the timpanist. They may be called kettledrums. Each can be tuned to a range of notes. Other drums used in the percussion section, such as the side drum, tenor drum and bass drum, are not tunable to a particular note.

Trombone   A brass instrument with a tube which can be altered in length by a sliding U-shaped section.

Trumpet   A brass instrument with three valves. There are several sizes.

Tuba The deepest-toned brass instrument, with three or four valves.

Violin family As well as the violin, the group includes the viola (slightly larger than the violin), 'cello (violoncello), and double bass.

A few instruments are used for special sound effects, such as the *tambourine*, a small drum with pairs of metal discs let into the frame and played by shaking and striking; *castanets*, two hollow wooden shells fastened by a cord passed over the thumb and first finger, which are played in pairs, one held in each hand and struck against one another, producing rhythmic clicks; *clappers*, a pair of woodblocks struck against one another; the *xylophone*, with a row of wooden bars struck with wooden hammers; the *vibraphone*, the same as the xylophone, but with metal bars, and usually struck with felt hammers.

As it is the violin which will probably be the focus of your own interest in the Suzuki methods of fostering talent, and as it will be that instrument which any Suzuki teacher will recommend, it is appropriate to outline the attractions both for your child and for you when choosing the best instrument for his musical education.

Suzuki's views were certainly affected by his own life-long delight in violin music. However, his preference is justified by sound practical knowledge of its advantages.

It is without doubt the musical instrument which most closely produces the sounds made by the human voice. It is capable of following vocal inflexions and tones so that, with very little practice and a minimum of training, it can be played to imitate the sounds which a child can make wordlessly.

Its long history shows how true this is, for some version of an instrument which has an infinite range of tone and notes has delighted mankind from very early times. Originally it was a pear-shaped instrument with a long tapering neck. It had two or three strings and was universally played by the peoples of the Middle East in the pre-Christian era. The unique feature compared with other primitive instruments was that the strings were stroked by a bow and not plucked. For generation after generation the art of making the rebec, as it was called, was passed down, along with the melodies which were not, of course, written.

As the traders and soldiers of mediaeval Europe travelled to the Arab world, they heard this instrument being played in villages and towns alike. A few were brought back, played and copied. By the early fifteenth century the rebec was being played for the entertainment of wealthy Venetian and Florentine merchants by strolling players who not only taught themselves to play, but often made their instruments.

Inventive ability developed the rebec into the viol, which was made in four sizes and had from five to seven strings. A century or so later quite different sizes and shapes were made, as can be seen today in the viola, violoncello and, of course, the violin. There are those who believe that the violin grew up from the same roots but was not a direct descendant of the viol. Suffice it to say that the violin family has a long and distinguished history.

Italian craftsmen vied with one another to perfect the violin. The most successful family were the Amati of Cremona in Italy. Their violins were basically of the same shape and size as the modern instrument. Stradivari, another of the Cremona craftsmen, made violins with a quality of sound which has never been surpassed.

To play the violin does not require physical strength beyond that of a small child, thanks to the fact that it is available in different sizes (quarter size and half size, for example). Contrary to the belief of those who have had no experience of violin playing, its weight is not supported by the left hand but is lodged between the chin and collar bone. In the case of a miniature violin, this hold presents no difficulty even to a three year-old child, provided the correct posture is taught.

As soon as actual playing is attempted, another technique will have to be learned: the use of the fingers of the left hand which control the notes by pressing different strings on the fingerboard. Accuracy in placing the fingers correctly is an essential skill and requires professional teaching.

A few teachers have suggested that, before any definite decision is taken about learning to play the violin, a young child can have his interest aroused by making him a 'pretend' violin. It can be made out of a reasonably strong cardboard box about 12 cms × 22 cms, stuffed with paper to retain its shape, and a piece of batten fixed with adhesive along the centre of the longer dimension of the box, one end flush with the edge and the other extending for about 10 cms. A 'pretend' bow cut from a length of bamboo can be added if this will stimulate the child's imagination. This idea should be no more than a very temporary one, just to interest the child in the possibility of holding the instrument between neck and shoulder, but it must not be a substitute for a real violin as the child can develop bad habits in holding it.

At least this 'pretend' violin will cost nothing and will give some clue to the child's genuine wish to play – an important factor if forcing a small child to start learning against his will is to be avoided. Not even the Suzuki system can succeed with a child who, for some reason (and usually it is the unconscious doubts of the parents) does not really want to make music.

The purchase of a violin (and do not forget that you

will need one for yourself if you intend to adopt the pupil-teacher role) will be quite costly. Most teachers do not want the child to own a violin until a few preliminary meetings have enabled them to assess his physical and mental development. They will then give advice on the most suitable size of instrument, pointing out that he will outgrow it and that you will need to replace it.

Really cheap violins, which are little more than toys, are quite useless. They are poorly made, break easily, and give the child no chance whatever of producing a pleasing sound. A violin of reasonable quality will cost upwards of £40–50, according to size. This is for a new instrument. Because of the need for larger sizes as a pupil grows and develops his ability, good quality second-hand instruments are probably the best solution and are usually available; any cost will in due course be lessened when the present violin is sold back to the dealer or is part-exchanged for a better one.

A bow is always included in the purchase price and will be perfectly suitable, so long as you go to a responsible music dealer and are not tempted by some instrument offered at a bargain price in a general second-hand store. Some rosin will also be included to use on the bow hairs.

There are many types of shoulder rest, ranging from a simple soft pad to an intricate wooden or metal structure. They are available in sizes to suit most sizes of instruments. The main use of the rest is to allow the player to get a good grip on the instrument without tension in the shoulder. A child's shoulder and collar bone are not covered with much flesh and it is important that a good grip is obtained without causing discomfort. The teacher will advise on this and will probably recommend a soft pad made with a piece of folded material padded with a few layers of tissue or spongy plastic.

The instrument and bow should be in a strong case. Generally the case is shaped to take the size of the instrument and is strongly made to withstand knocks sustained during carrying and general handling.

The other members of the violin family are too large for a very small child to play. But the principles involved in playing them are naturally the same as for the violin and many young Suzuki pupils change to the viola, 'cello, or even the double bass after some years of their Suzuki violin course.

The second most popular instrument for Suzuki pupils is the pianoforte. The child must be old enough to be able to sit comfortably on a raised stool and have a sufficient length of arm and fingers to reach the notes.

Parents are attracted to the idea of the piano rather than the violin as a medium for their child's musical education for all sorts of reasons. The two generally mentioned to me are that the ability to play the piano is a social asset and, secondly, that the family possesses a piano which at least one adult member of the family knows how to play. A less frequent reason is that, next to singing, playing the piano is the most promising talent for a career bringing fame and fortune.

It is true enough that anyone who can play the piano with reasonable ability will give himself and his family a lot of pleasure in the home and will be welcomed at many a party. And a piano-owning family will save the expense of buying an instrument for the Suzuki pupil. As regards the vision of a glittering and lucrative career on the concert platform, the chances are slim indeed. Admittedly there are more public performances by solo pianists than by any other instrumental soloists, but it is worth pointing out that only a comparatively small number of orchestral pieces, apart from some concertos, include a piano, while the typical symphony orchestra may include anything from ten to twenty violinists. Virtually all smaller combinations playing classical music include one or more violins or instruments in the violin family.

In any event, regarding a course of Suzuki-style tuition as a way to produce a professional musician in the family is the wrong attitude. Suzuki's intention is not to discover child prodigies or train boys and girls who will in due course become professional musicians. Probably only one in a hundred children taught under Suzuki methods takes up the violin professionally in the late teens. The rest develop into happy, intelligent and psychologically healthy youngsters, which is Suzuki's intention.

If the choice of instrument for your child is the piano you are possibly biased because you own one. The only expenditure will be having it tuned, ideally three times a year. It is also important to see that the action of the piano is in good order, or all kinds of bad habits may be learned through inequalities of pressure between different notes. If the piano is old it may not hold a proper overall pitch. This will hamper your child's musical development, as he will have difficulty in adjusting from the pitch of your piano to any other.

During tuition, your child will not enjoy the company of fellow pupils because group classes with more than one child playing at any given time are not feasible without a costly electronic system of linked keyboards. Nor will it be easy to find a Suzuki-trained teacher who has had a course in piano teaching and who has these facilities. In the essential practice at home you will not be able to play simultaneously with your child, except in a duet version, but will have to take each piece in turn. Unless you do this you will be abandoning the ideal of being a fellow pupil and not just a supervisor.

All that said, if you remain determined that the piano shall be your child's instrument, do not be deterred by the problems. They are not insuperable, as many parents have proved, and there is a teaching method published which is based on Suzuki's ideas.

Now for some of the other instruments which may seem attractive to your child, and which can be taught with most of the Suzuki ideas maintained.

Many children who have reached the school age of five years will be taught the recorder. It is a musical instrument older in origin even than the violin. Recorder-type instruments made from animal bones and hollow pieces of wood have been found all over the world. They can be thousands of years old, dating from the time when primitive man discovered that by humming or singing into a hollow tube he could improve the resulting sound. Then he found that by making some holes in the tube he could produce a melody, simply by blowing and closing one hole or another with his finger tips.

The recorder is an inexpensive instrument to buy as an extra possession, encouraging a child to create music for himself. It requires very little lung pressure to produce the notes.

The 'big brother' of the recorder is the flute. Children of eight years and upwards who have become moderately skilled on a recorder can progress to the flute without difficulty, although the flute is demanding physically and requires lung control which a child who is a shallow breather will find tiring. Conscientious teachers will check a child's physique by getting a medical opinion before teaching him to play a flute. There is a flute method published, based on the Suzuki system, and devised in collaboration with Dr Suzuki.

These precautions about too early adoption of the flute also apply to the clarinet, oboe, bassoon, and saxophone.

Physical factors also apply to the consideration of brass instruments. Boy Scouts and similar organisations have made the bugle popular, unfortunately usually without much regard for the quality of the tone, even though it is simple to play. Many children, particularly in the North of England, progress from bugle blowing to the cornet, giving them an interest which can take them on to membership of a brass band; many of these have a very high standard of musicianship and provide a hobby which will last a lifetime.

When the bugler moves on to the trumpet, he has advanced well beyond any rudimentary technique. The skill requires expert tuition and ceaseless practice, as with all instruments. A teaching programme should not begin too early because the vibration of the mouthpiece against the lips can permanently and prematurely toughen them. Moreover, the need for a correct breathing technique can be beyond the physical powers of a young boy and cause dizziness if playing is not interrupted with regular rest periods. It is, of course, possible to begin to learn to play a cornet or trumpet without first beginning on a bugle.

Lastly, there is the modern innovation of the electronic keyboard, comparatively cheap when compared with a piano. Clever advertising has claimed that it is quite simple to play and attractive to all members of the family, young or old. A good one with touch differentiation (the harder the key is pressed the louder the note) is almost as expensive as a conventional piano and far more liable to defects in use, requiring servicing and repairs.

If the aim is to teach a child the piano, only a teacher who is fascinated by the possibilities of playing an electronically controlled instrument while somehow retaining a regard for the principles of Suzuki tuition is likely to agree to teach on this specialised instrument. Assuming the pupil's real ambition is to become a pianist, he will eventually have to have a conventional piano instead of the electronic version.

To sum up this survey of musical instruments for the tuition of very young children, the best advice is to opt for the violin or piano at this time, but have a further look at others, either as a second instrument or as a principal one, as your child becomes physically more developed.

6   From Solo to Group Activities

So far we have assumed that your interest and practical moves in preparing your child for professional Suzuki tuition have been restricted to the family circle. In the early stages that is undoubtedly the best policy, but as soon as your child is old enough to enjoy the companionship of other children of much the same age, it will greatly help to contact their parents and talk to them.

You will certainly know of many boys and girls of the same age as your child, and you have probably struck up a friendship with their parents. It will be quite unusual if these friends know much about Suzuki education, beyond being briefly interested while watching a TV performance of tiny Japanese children all playing violins with obvious pleasure and considerable talent.

The precision of their performance and the ritualistic bowing at the start and finish of their playing can give the uninformed the idea that it is all a purely Japanese ceremony; the children have, they rather suspect, been moulded into precocious performers to produce an entertainment highly profitable to the promoters.

In reality, organising a score of small Japanese children, along with their mothers or guardians, on an international tour is an expensive project and not undertaken for financial gain. Suzuki knows from years of experience that demonstrating what children can do without cajoling or forcing is an effective way of arousing serious interest in his methods throughout the world.

In chatting to other mothers at a child clinic, play-school or when you meet out shopping, you will have noted those whose devotion to their children is as great as yours. Let them know just what you have been doing with music as an educational tool; invite one or two to bring their children to your home for morning coffee or tea in the afternoon; see if the children seem to get on well with one another. If your child can show off a little by choosing a cassette or record and putting it on the machine, the other children will be envious and their mothers quietly impressed.

It will not be easy to explain Suzuki's theories and methods during an informal chat, and you don't want to appear to be giving a lecture. If their interest is obvious, you could lend them this book or any of the Suzuki publications mentioned at the end of the book. Any of your friends who have been genuinely intrigued by the idea will soon want to talk things over with you.

The upshot could well be that your music listening sessions will no longer always be a private activity for your child and yourself, but for a group of two or three children and their parents, sometimes in your home and sometimes in that of your child's new friends.

These meetings may be quite infrequent, for you should not overdo it with a rigid schedule. If you do, your friends may become annoyed at such interruptions to their routine and the children may grow bored with one another. So long as the visits to one home or another occur irregularly, the children will look on them as a treat and their mothers will enjoy developing friendships.

I know of successful Suzuki groups which had their origin in this modest beginning, spreading from a couple of families as word of mouth explanations brought in a dozen more, the music sessions growing into an informal children's party. One or two dropped out, but always one or two more joined. There is something about the enthusiasm of Suzuki's methods which is infectious.

The earlier you can start this co-operative effort on a preparatory programme of listening, the better will be your chances of getting help in classes and from a professional teacher. The first thing to do is to write for details of any classes in your area to the British Suzuki Institute, 21 London Road, St Albans, Hertfordshire, AL1 1LQ. Mention the number of children who would be students. Such classes are at present not numerous, but that need not prevent you from investigating other possibilities of getting a class started.

If you can show that there are ten or a dozen parents who would send their children to regular music teaching sessions based on Suzuki methods, your local authority will be more inclined to take notice than it would if you were just a solitary enquirer. You can support your ideas with the help of voluntary groups which are interested in musical education for children and children's welfare generally.

You may be lucky enough to live in an area where the local education authority does organise music classes which have adopted the Suzuki system, although pupils will have to be old enough to go to school – i.e. four to five years. Such classes are comparatively rare, but there will be no harm in asking for Suzuki-style lessons to be organised, or at least for enquiries to be made about the existence of Suzuki-trained teachers among the existing staff.

Obstacles which will probably be raised fall under three main headings. First, the time involved. The usual scheme for early teaching is to take about four pupils at a time for a half-hour session. At first the desirable policy is on a one-to-one basis, say just five to ten minutes of individual tuition for one child while the others look on.

After some weeks each child will need up to twenty minutes' personal attention, so that only three pupils are actually learning and watching in an hour's session. Thus more staff and more time are needed for a Suzuki class than for a conventional one.

This creates financial problems at a time when economies are essential in the education service. Not only is the teacher-pupil ratio high, but if children have to be taught as soon as they start schooling, it means the school has to provide teaching facilities two or three years earlier than would be the case in conventional music tuition, which usually starts when children are seven or eight.

A second problem which some schools adopting Suzuki teaching methods have experienced is that the very success of the method means an additional demand on teaching staff's time. Records kept over many years have shown that a considerable percentage of pupils taught by conventional methods drop out after a few years. But the drop-out rate with Suzuki pupils is far less, and the number of children who continue to want to learn becomes greater as time passes, once more increasing school expenditure.

Difficulties over financial and staffing problems are not insuperable, as many schools up and down the country have proved. With good will and patience on the part of education committees, school staff and parents, Suzuki groups can be started, just as they are for many other ancillary scholastic activities, such as drama, overseas trips, and sports.

The matter of staff numbers is not really a factor for parents to worry about, nor indeed is it something they can do much to solve. But it will help to realise that a local authority usually has a fixed number of teachers with the expertise to teach music. More often than not, their methods will be based on conventional ideas. To have them trained in Suzuki methods is rather like asking a teacher of French to change to teaching Spanish or Italian. He or she has a flair for languages and would not find such a change impossible, but not at the cost of discarding French.

A third problem you will be told about is the necessary adaptation of the school's routine. A room has to be made available for the Suzuki music lessons at which parents accompany their children; other teachers will have to organise timing so that two or three children can periodically leave their classroom for the Suzuki music lesson without missing the basic class lesson and disrupting class discipline.

Local education authorities are not required to provide teaching facilities for children below school age, nor additions to any existing procedures for teaching a given subject. But they may do so if they accept that there is a genuine need in the local community, and that the number of parents is large enough to make such an additional facility viable. That is why it will help if you can speak for ten or more other parents. You can then counter any suggestion that there is little or no demand for musical education outside the standard school programme. If you can persuade your local councillor to back you, that will also help.

It must be conceded that, beyond those local education authorities which have already adopted the Suzuki teaching system, the most promising source of help will be in private groups and from individual teachers. Quite unknown to you, there may be such a group within reasonable travelling distance of your own home. Your local main library will keep lists of the names and addresses of groups and organisations whose members are involved in amateur dramatics, concerts, choral singing, folk dancing, and so on, as well as those concerned with children's welfare and recreations such as ballet. At the very least, these people can give you details of available accommodation in a spacious room or hall, and all of them will include people who are keen to promote the cultural interests of children.

Of the five thousand children studying under fully or partly Suzuki-trained teachers in Britain in the 1980s, it is estimated that more than half of them have had most of their lessons in the home of one of the parents, in a spare room of a local music college, or in a room hired by the hour from a youth organisation such as the Scouts or Guides.

During your search for help in inaugurating a new Suzuki group, after accepting that none exists in your district, you will be meeting people who are acquainted with the private teaching facilities that already exist. Early on you should contact them to see if they have experience of Suzuki methods. Local music shops often know of teachers. The Yellow Pages of the telephone directory list both music shops and music teachers under Music. All large public libraries are supplied with an annual list issued by the Incorporated Society of Musicians in a register of private teachers. The list gives names of private teachers by area and type of instrument taught. Not all teachers are members of the above Society so it is worth asking the librarian for a list of local music societies and associations; they can invariably provide the names and addresses of teachers.

It will not be too difficult to find a music teacher, but much harder to get hold of one who has been Suzuki-trained or at least has had experience of the methods and has read all the books he or she can obtain which explain both the Suzuki philosophy and its programme of tuition. Don't be tempted to consider a teacher who claims the old conventional methods are just as good.

How can you recognise a good Suzuki teacher? First of all she – and generally speaking a woman teacher is more likely to be available when pre-school children are to be taught – will want to meet you, your friends and the children. Informal meetings in your home can be the introduction so that everyone, parents and children alike, feel that they can be friends with her.

Every mother and child will know instinctively if the teacher really loves children. This is almost as important as evidence of her ability and skill. The title of Suzuki's best known book on his Talent Education theories is *Nurtured by Love*, and he puts a loving approach to the pupil before deep knowledge. If, at these preliminary meetings, the teacher gives a general outline of Suzuki teaching, you will be able to gauge how suitable she is by her enthusiasm and accounts of her experience. This is more important than details of any degrees the teacher obtained as a student.

She will want to know how much listening to music both mothers and children have enjoyed; if you have already followed the routine described earlier in this book she will be both impressed and relieved, knowing that the progress which can be achieved without professional aid has been attained.

The starting age may come up for discussion. Some teachers regard age five as the ideal starting time, some are unwilling to accept them at three or four, and some are dubious about children well past their fifth year. But few observe a rigid attitude to the precise age. Much depends on the child's signs of growing maturity: is he too small to cope, or too old to mix well with children considerably younger than he is?

The ideal teacher will prefer to start lessons for the mother, with the child just watching. This will mean about eight weekly lessons, and she will be able to take four adults at a time. At about the sixth lesson – when the mother will be surprised how well she is able to play in tune – the teacher will not object if any of the children want to take part by playing on a 'pretend' violin, although they will not yet be given much instruction beyond how to hold the imitation violin and bow correctly. Then, after the eight lessons for mothers, the children will be ready for their first real tuition.

Private tuition is not cheap. Some teachers charge per lesson, some by a term of lessons corresponding roughly to the three terms of schools. Obviously there can be some adjustment if she teaches a group of, say, four children, instead of one, and most teachers really prefer to teach a group so that the children become accustomed to playing with their little friends.

As a rough guide, the teacher's fee will work out at £6–£10 per hour. This sum is, of course, shared among the parents, so that, in the usual preliminary of teaching four mothers, the cost to each will be between £1.50 and £2.50. But as the lesson time increases to 20 minutes per child, the cost will increase proportionately and in later years half and three-quarter hour lessons will be needed.

7 First Class with Suzuki

Let's assume that you, the mother (although there are instances where the father is the partner because he is regarded as the real music lover in the family, or because he can better adapt his routine to attend classes), have completed your preparations either to become a pupil or to take the necessary active and interested part in your child's lessons.

Now the real Suzuki class is about to start. Accept right away that you will be much more nervous and tense than your child. If he is under five years old he will be eager to learn to play a violin properly and will have plenty of confidence.

Dr David Weikart, President of the American High School Educational Foundation which also trains educational leaders in Britain, has suggested in a wide survey that pre-school age education is an invaluable start in fostering intelligence. Moreover, he discovered that children enjoy attending a class at an age which conventional opinion considers too early.

'At the age of four,' says Dr Weikart, 'the child is beginning to feel comfortable for the first time in circumstances outside the home. They are at an age when they can still trust; they haven't developed a mistrust of things that are going to happen so they develop a willingness to respond.'

As you set off for the first class, your child will be

carrying his first real violin, bought, one hopes, after seeking the advice of the teacher. She will have dealt with any problems you may have had with this vital and, admittedly, quite costly part of the teaching programme.

Typical of the queries parents raise with teachers are:

1   *Is a miniature violin essential? Isn't this tiny one just a toy? My child is growing so fast that surely it won't be long before a 'proper' full-sized one is needed? Couldn't that be used from the start? After all, he will soon grow into it.*

The answer is that on balance it would be better for the child a year or two hence to be playing a too-small violin than to start now with a too-large one. To present a small child, embarking on his Suzuki lessons, with a violin too large for him, is to turn a desired possession into a disappointment. The child will find it tiring to hold for the required length of practice and accurate placing of the fingers will be difficult.

You can make a simple test at the music shop when buying a violin. When the child is given the instrument to hold, his left arm should have a natural bend at the elbow and should not be stretched along the back of the instrument because his arm is too short to permit any bending. The angle at the elbow should be great enough to allow the wrist to be in a straight line with the forearm and not bent in an effort to help support the instrument.

And don't forget the bow. Usually this is sold with the violin, but it should not be accepted just because the violin seems suitable. Once you yourself have had some initial tuition, you will know that the bow is almost as important as the violin itself. The first thing to check is that it is the right size for your child. Secondly, it should have a straight stick. As the bow is under tension, controlled by a screw at one end, there is a risk that, if it has been badly stored in the shop, it will have developed a curve towards the tip. The result of this is that it will be impossible to draw a straight bow over the strings.

If the violin and bow are cheaper than other models of the same size on offer, it may be that the band of hair on the bow is narrower than it should be. Too few hairs are the cause of poor tone.

2   *Can't I rent a small violin if it will be needed for only a short time?*

The answer is yes – in some shops. But it usually means that it has been previously rented out, perhaps several times. It also means that you are giving your child a second- or third-hand instrument which has probably been subjected to rough handling on occasion. Rather than trying to rent an instrument, check with the dealer that he will be willing to part-exchange it for a larger instrument in due course. He will invariably be ready to do this because it will mean a further sale in the future. If the small violin costs about £40–50, as it may, you should be able to arrange for a deduction of about £30 on the part-exchange deal if the violin and bow are in good condition. Renting one will involve a total of about £35 a year payable in monthly instalments, and at the end of the hiring period you will of course own nothing. If you must spread the cost, it would be better to sign a hire-purchase agreement, even though the interest would increase the total payment considerably.

Don't forget a small square of soft material to fold and use as a shoulder pad. You can buy shoulder pads, but they are not always necessary as a home-made one can be tailored to the most comfortable area and thickness. Some teachers regard pads as essential, others do not. It is possible to hold the violin without one if the child is properly taught and the general balance of his posture is good.

A friendly atmosphere at the class is all-important. The teacher will know how to greet small children and make them feel they are welcome. A few minutes for the children to meet one another, plus some talk among the mothers, will create the right atmosphere for what is to be more of a game than a strictly regimented lesson.

Teachers' methods vary. A typical early stage is for a beginner to have some general instruction on holding the violin and bow and on standing without strain. Small children have a short concentration ability and an actual lesson will not last more than five minutes for each child. He can then relax and watch the other pupils have their lesson before he again has a five-minute session.

During this period, the parents can sit around watching and helping their own children. Teachers dislike parents huddling together and having a gossip; they are expected to maintain their role as both pupils and assistant teachers. By watching and listening they will gain useful hints on how to continue practising what their children have learned that day.

Before your child is encouraged to see if he can extract a sound with his bow drawn across the strings, the teacher will help him to hold both violin and bow correctly. She may stand behind him and place her hands over his, proving to him that he can produce one or two notes from his violin. She will also help him to adopt the correct posture, with the feet slightly apart and turned outwards, taking the body's weight equally on both legs to ensure that there is no strain or stress.

Some teachers follow the Japanese idea of giving each pupil a sheet of strong paper or cardboard, marked with his name and outlines of his feet in the correct position. No young child can be expected to stand still for very long, but the idea of having a picture of his feet, and of soon being able to recognise his own name on the card, will make him eager to pick up his own piece of paper or cardboard, put it on the floor, and stand on it ready for his lesson.

If it is possible for a full-length mirror to be brought to the class, this will be of great help in encouraging the child, both in holding the violin and bow correctly and in adopting the correct posture. Children love looking at themselves.

The next step is to prepare the child for playing, showing him how to place the first, second and third fingers of his left hand on the A string and to hold the bow so that the hair just touches the string. As most mothers should have learned this procedure in preliminary sessions with the teacher, they will probably have encouraged their child to make this preparatory routine at home on the 'pretend' violin. In any case he will not find it difficult to imitate.

Twinkle, twinkle, little star is the universally adopted tune for young beginners. Apart from the simple and delightful melody, they enjoy the rhyme for which the tune was written; it has been sung and recited by children for generations. In the Suzuki programme the tune is used for a series of rhythmical exercises which will convince any child of the possibilities for developing different sounds from even the simplest of melodies. The teacher will play some of the variations on *Twinkle* just to show the pupils what they, in time, will also be able to play.

As Suzuki pupils do not have to read music and know the letters of notes simply from the teacher mentioning them as she plays them, learning depends entirely on the child's natural means of communication – seeing and hearing. He can see the position of the bow on the strings and its movement. He can hear the result of that movement, and he will want to imitate it.

His first efforts to copy the teacher's movements will inevitably be a failure, although he will almost certainly produce a sound, so proving to himself that a violin can indeed be used to make a noise. Some small children have the dexterity – or have absorbed knowledge from watching their mothers – to get the right note after two or three attempts. Repetition will bring improvement, and then the first five-minute session will be over. The child will not completely forget how he played the successful note and he will be able to repeat it when he practises it at home or later in the lesson.

Not all children will enjoy this minor triumph during the first lesson. Their co-ordination between mind and muscle may still be poor. Any small child is bound to be aware that the few notes he manages to produce are not quite what he heard when the teacher played them. He will try again if he is encouraged rather than criticised. 'That was quite good and it shows you can learn to play; let's do it once more after listening to teacher's playing,' will be more effective than a half-joking comment such as, 'My word, that wasn't too good, was it? You couldn't have been really listening to teacher.'

Generally, it is better if the mother keeps quiet during the class lesson, leaving any comment to the teacher. The mother can talk about the child's playing later, when they have a mutual rehearsal at home.

It has to be realised that the delicate movements to be made when playing a violin are difficult enough even for a physically mature and trained player. There are few musical instruments which are affected so sensitively by every movement as the violin. Small children's reactions which I have observed in class instruction have varied from difficulty in imitating the actions demonstrated to them, resulting in tantrums and tears, to an obstinate persistence in trying to produce the desired note, when they are clearly not bothering to heed the teacher's advice.

A good teacher will deal with such a crisis very gently indeed. She will suspect that the temporary setback is the fault of the parent or herself, and not of the child. She will not mislead the child by telling him that he is doing quite nicely when the child is all too aware that he is not, nor will she go to the other extreme and reprove him with some such remark as, 'You haven't been listening to what I said, and didn't watch me carefully when I played the note.'

She will deal with the trouble by suggesting, 'I don't think you were holding the bow quite right and the violin isn't comfy on your shoulder. Let's see if we can find a better way.' Then she will stand behind the child, place her hands over his as she did in the very first lesson, but remove them before he actually draws the bow across the strings. A mother should watch this 'first aid' routine carefully, so that she can adopt it during the child's practices at home.

At this point, one should mention that it is a good idea to keep a combined notebook and diary, recording notes about the teacher's comments, answers to any questions you may have put to her, and a summary of what your child did at each lesson. Later, at home, you can jot down any queries you may have and take them up with the teacher at the next lesson.

Sometimes parents may feel indignant about a teacher's insistence on repetition, when to them it seems that their child has mastered one simple movement. Apart from the fact that constantly repeating every note is a keystone of Suzuki teaching, the teacher may have detected a fault in technique which has to be remedied. To ignore the need for expert observation may result in a child adopting chronically bad habits. Suzuki himself always stresses that the years he spent teaching himself produced so many errors in his technique that he had eventually to accept that he could never be the skilled player of professional standard which had been his ambition. That is why the parent should restrict instruction at home to a back-up of the teacher's methods. A notebook recording what the teacher said and did will be an invaluable guide.

Additional aids for home use in support of the teacher's class come in the form of tape cassettes and the Suzuki Books. The books are numbered 1–10, covering the entire course of tuition as far as the age group of 12 plus. Book 1 begins with *Twinkle, twinkle, little star*, as in the first class lessons. It is important that, when you play the tape and follow the book material during your daily practice at home, you do not advance past the stage reached in the class. The teacher will advise you on how much tape to play and what to read from the book.

Early on in the course, the teacher will hold a group lesson. There is a variety of methods which she can adopt. Some have a group session after each child's individual lesson; others make it a special lesson lasting the whole period at three- or four-week intervals. It will depend on whether the number of pupils in the group consists of ten or more children, but the concept of group playing can be followed with only three or four players.

The advantage of group practising is that it encourages a child to play as well as the others and it inculcates knowledge of timing. Group playing helps to develop friendships and is a certain method of curing shyness which often inhibits a small child if he is the sole focus of attention.

Once Suzuki classes have started they must be attended regularly unless illness or some unavoidable event occurs. The success of the Suzuki method depends entirely on memory, and to imprint its teaching in the mind repetition and regular mental refreshment are essential. This also applies to the parallel practising at home, not only by the child, but by the mother, too. She must never forget that she is her child's fellow-pupil. If she skimps the practice period, her child will also want to do so. If she drops out of attending every class, persuading a friend to take her child to the class, her child will find reasons to drop out and stay at home.

Practising the lesson at home, once professional instruction has been given, will obviously be possible much more frequently than at a class (daily home practice is the ideal) and Suzuki believes that the home is a richer source of progress than the classroom.

When the time comes for lessons to start, not even preliminary talks with the prospective teacher can entirely satisfy the doubts and worries of the average conscientious mother; she is probably also being besieged with more or less unanswerable questions from her child. The Suzuki system is so novel and, in Britain, so little known or understood, that such misgivings are inevitable.

Ideally, your child will be joining an established project, and both mother and child can be invited just to come to a lesson and see what happens. But in most districts that privilege will be unlikely.

Here is a general description of the routine at a typical early class, held in this instance in a London district.

It is a group lesson, combining two classes – five children (two boys and three girls) with an average age of five who started their lessons two months previously, and six children (four girls and two boys) in their second term of instruction. None of the mothers had learned the violin in their own childhood. Four of them had had some lessons in playing the piano.

The room is in a Memorial Hall, with facilities for a variety of local activities, large or small. In the room is an upright piano (a permanent fixture) which the teacher may occasionally use to help the pupils appreciate different notes struck separately.

The teacher is there to welcome the children; she has

already learned their names and something about their family circumstances. She chats briefly to what she calls her senior pupils, the mothers, while the children rather warily mix with the strangers of the other group. Their mothers move to the chairs around the room and help the children to remove the violins and bows from their cases. Taking good care of them was the first instruction the children were given, along with the names of the various parts of both violin and bow.

The teacher explains what they will all be doing in the next hour. In this case it is to play *Twinkle, twinkle* in a group of eleven, all keeping the same time. Then she helps all the children to loosen up and get to know one another by walking round the room, changing their places by naming two children at a time, and finally telling them to pick up their violins and range themselves in the middle of the room. Meanwhile the mothers have got their own violins ready.

Before actual playing begins, the teacher demonstrates how to hold the bow. She does this at the start of every lesson. Suzuki sets great store by correct holding, at first concentrating on short strokes which can eradicate the discordant scraping which any new pupil is prone to produce. Next she checks posture – body weight evenly distributed on both legs and a straight line from the chin to the left foot.

When playing begins, the teacher helps any child having difficulty by standing behind him, placing her hands over his and moving the bow and fingers correctly.

Playing is not stopped too frequently, so that the children can hear for themselves that the tune is not as it should be. Successful players are praised, but offenders are not reproved. The latter will be perfectly aware of their mistakes, and they will then consciously try to copy the pupils who are praised.

Periods of playing, unless the results are very good, last only two or three minutes, with rests in between when the teacher can comment on the performance and demonstrate the next sequence. By the end of the lesson the group will have played a recognisable part, or even all, of *Twinkle, twinkle*, and their minds will have indelibly recorded every movement involved, so that they will be able to repeat each one when they practise at home.

In this class, as in many, the teacher has a cassette recording of *Twinkle, twinkle* played by more advanced pupils. Her final procedure is to play this through for the children to hear. She promises them that as soon as they can play it as well as that, she will bring a microphone and tape recorder to the class so they can be on tape, too.

8 The Suzuki Books

The entire programme of Suzuki violin teaching is based on ten Books which take the student through a complete course. Book 10 will bring him to a standard of performance acceptable for admission to colleges of music with students approved for a professional career in music. By the Suzuki method of teaching a student may reach this level at the age of twelve, which will mean he has at least five years to develop his technique before college education and possible attainment of a musical degree. The piece used in Book 10 is Mozart's D Major Concerto, which, as anyone with knowledge of music will know, presents a challenge even to a professional violinist.

That the ten Books describe the teaching programme from *Twinkle, twinkle, little star* in Book 1 to this Mozart masterpiece in Book 10 will indicate how complete the teaching programme is for any youngster who becomes so enthralled with violin playing that a professional career is envisaged. But it should once more be stressed that, while professional standards are there for the determined, they are not the goal for the average young person.

About one out of every hundred past Suzuki students has taken up violin playing as a career, or even wanted to do so. Only a comparatively small proportion of pupils continue with the Suzuki programme as far as Book 10.

Most are happy when they have learned enough to play with satisfaction to themselves and can participate in school and, later, amateur adult orchestras.

All this is said by way of warning to parents who enthusiastically purchase all ten Books at once, intrigued by the thought that their child, who has only just started to learn the rudiments of violin playing, will, in the remarkably short time of six or seven years, emerge as a budding Yehudi Menuhin or Kyung Wha Chung. Not only is the child far too young to be assessed as exceptionally blessed with something more than just talent, but his parents may be tempted to force him to work harder at his practising. What Suzuki intends to be a satisfying pleasure may degenerate into a burdensome task. Anyway, the teacher will not approve, and she will not devote extra attention to one child when her policy is equality of care and attention for all her pupils.

The most sensible course, as your child begins Suzuki tuition, is to restrict your purchase to Books 1 and 2 (along with their accompanying cassettes or records). The teacher will doubtless give you all the details on cost and source of supply. She may well be able to order them for you, and even have second-hand copies under an arrangement to buy them back from students who are older and are using Book 3 onwards. If the class is small you may come to an arrangement to share the Books among two or three mothers, although this is not very satisfactory since they really have to be referred to at home as well as during the class lessons.

Ideally you should acquire Books 1 and 2, plus the appropriate recordings, as soon as you have fixed the date for starting class lessons, so that you can study the contents. You will also be able to play the recordings of the early pieces to give both your child and yourself a good idea of what will happen at the lesson. These recordings should be played daily, enabling your child to become familiar with the tunes. They will then be well memorised and will make it easier for the child to recognise the tune he is being taught to play on his violin. Whatever time you choose for this daily recital – during meals, after an outing to the shops or playtime outside the home – be sure also to play it just before you set off for the class. This will ensure that the music is in the forefront of your child's memory.

At first sight the contents of Book 1 – and, of course, all the other Books – will appear both formidable and confusing to a reader with very little musical knowledge. They will be much easier to understand once the Suzuki-trained teacher has given lessons based on the contents. Her actual demonstration of the Book's descriptive material will solve all your queries, and will incidentally show that it is virtually impossible to attempt some kind of do-it-yourself modification of the Suzuki programme at home and without professional help and advice.

The Books will give you a general idea of the manner in which a child, with absolutely no knowledge of playing music, is led steadily to a standard of performance rarely attained by conventional methods and certainly not in such a short period.

There is no point at this stage in giving a detailed description of all the Books which cover Suzuki teaching over an indefinite period. An outline of the contents of Book 1 will suffice to indicate what a child will learn in the first year or eighteen months, the duration depending on the frequency of the lessons.

Most teachers divide the tuition covered by Book 1 into three levels. Level 1 consists of five pieces: *Twinkle, twinkle* and its variations, plus some folk music. Level 2: *May Song* and exercise pieces by Suzuki. Level 3: three minuets by Bach and a gavotte by Gossec.

Given regular classes and daily practising at home, all

these tunes will be played with some degree of ability within eighteen months from the beginning of class teaching. Inevitably there will be mistakes and omissions now and then, but no child will forget what he has repeatedly heard, just as he learned to speak through hearing words over and over again. As in the case of speech, when there is no question of 'you have learned those words; now we needn't say them again but can start learning new words', so the pieces of music learned from Book 1 are not dropped but continue to be part of the learning programme, being constantly improved as skill develops. Suzuki has claimed that he can tell which Book a pupil has reached simply by listening to him playing *Twinkle, twinkle.*

By the time a child has learned all the pieces in Book 1, playing them will take about 20 minutes, including brief rests and some repetition. The last piece, Gossec's gavotte, is the link to the pieces in Book 2. In this Book more emphasis is put on expression and, in addition, more time is spent on group practice. This will highlight any differences in the children's progress and introduce a degree of competition, which is no bad thing. The younger and less advanced child will be eager to emulate the more accomplished pupil, while the latter will be encouraged to retain his place as one of the good players so that he does not 'lose face'.

Book 2's exercises enable the 'grammar' of a piece of music to be taught. The teacher will explain that every piece of music consists of phrases, brief and largely independent, just as in speech sentences indicate pauses, changes of subject and so on in the overall vocal expression.

Producing the musical phrases in a piece of music so as to be audible to the player and listener, is part of the teaching in Book 2. The method of achieving this technique requires a teacher's instruction. A slight change of direction of the bow, perhaps only a millimetre or so, and a slight cessation of bow movement, are among the means of improvement the teacher will explain. Depending on the frequency of the lessons, the average pupil will have absorbed the tuition based on this book in eighteen months to two years from the commencement of the classes.

A small proportion of children drop out at this time, when they are seven or eight years old. This can occasionally be a parental decision, but more usually it is due to the fact that school activities – which may well include conventional music teaching and plans to form a school orchestra – demand the child's contribution.

Whatever his future pattern of activities, the child who has successfully completed the lessons covered by Books 1 and 2 will have gained knowledge he will never forget. The fundamental aim of Suzuki's scheme to develop general talent and create a love of music will have been achieved.

The intention of this book has been to introduce parents to the potentialities of Suzuki Talent Education. It will at this stage suffice to give a general outline of the teaching involved in long-term education involved in books 3–10.

Book 3 introduces the pupil to a standard of sophisticated performance which would be too difficult for a young player without thorough grounding in the lessons of the previous two Books. The musical quality of the set pieces is stressed, with the aim of creating a confident technique and an accurate ear. The sensitivity in the composer's work is brought out, supported by the pupil's own educated insight and by the teacher's explanation and example in playing the pieces.

Book 4 brings the opportunity to tackle concerto movements. Many teachers regard the Vivaldi Concerto in A Minor as the watershed of the entire Suzuki course.

When the pupil can play this concerto it will indicate that he has mastered the basic technique and appreciates the composer's intentions. A player who has learned to admire a piece by Vivaldi can regard himself as a true lover of superb music. Vivaldi, who was taught to play the violin by his father, a violinist at St Mark's in Venice, wrote some 450 concertos, mostly for instruments in the violin family, as well as 73 sonatas for one or two violins. Thus any student intrigued by Vivaldi compositions has an almost inexhaustible supply of pieces to play for his own pleasure and, if his ambitions lead that way, as a professional soloist.

The remaining six Books are designed to permit a more flexible approach to suit the individual student's needs. By then, unless the parents have practical knowledge of advanced techniques, their involvement in contributing to the teaching scheme is less vital. By the time Book 5 is reached the teacher will be identifying each pupil's preferences in his choice of music, and there will be a degree of specialisation. The teacher's experience will enable her to select a programme of music technically within the student's knowledge and with due regard for his preferences.

Whether a course of Suzuki violin teaching right through to Book 10 will irresistibly tempt the by now accomplished student to hope for a professional career, depends on his determination to adopt music for a livelihood. His teacher will be able to give both him and his family an objective assessment of the possibilities. She will point out that it will mean further education and years of unremitting study and practice, followed by intense competition to make a living.

This fulfilment is not really the purpose of Suzuki's scheme. If the student, after years of study and practice taking him well into adolescence, has enriched his life with a love of music, that will be reward enough. His family can be proud of him as a well-rounded human being, and he will have an interest which will be with him for the rest of his life, no matter what career he adopts.

9 Reading Music the Suzuki Way

A question that always arises when parents consider Suzuki musical education for their children is, 'When are pupils taught to read music?'

Their reaction when told that, certainly for the first year or so, they are not formally taught how to read the notes on sheet music or in the Books, is one of doubt and disappointment. Many remember the ritual of reciting EGBDF and FACE, identifying them on a blackboard or in an exercise book, and then facing all the mysteries of sharps and flats, etcetera. It was invariably a long, long time before they could play even a rudimentary one-finger tune on a piano.

It was left to Suzuki to point out the simple fact that every child on earth learns to speak words and then reasonably fluent phrases without the knowledge to identify single letters, let alone their combination to make words.

If, in some far-fetched fictional story, a Tarzan-type human being, child or adult, taught himself language by looking at printed words, it is just within the realms of possibility that he might in time make sense of it. But he would certainly be unable to turn the received information into sounds any one else could understand. To speak coherently he would have to hear the words as well as see them in a letter code of literacy.

Suzuki prefers to put first things first. He uses the

power of imitation supported by memory. He has shown that from early babyhood sounds are absorbed, memorised and in due time imitated, whether to speak or to add melody to the voice. When it comes to playing an instrument to make music, physical skills are required, none of which are instinctive movements but have to be learned. This dexterity needs concentration, and if the main purpose is to imitate or produce a desired sound, success is much more likely than it would be if the instructional code on a sheet of music had to be solved. Suzuki postpones reading music until the musical memory and the ability to handle a violin successfully have been developed.

Only by imitating a musical sound stored in the aural memory can there be real feeling and sensitivity – the almost indescribable assets which nevertheless are so obvious in performance. They mean the difference between a piece played by a skilled pianist and the same tune strummed on an old-fashioned fairground piano. Both pieces are note-perfect; the difference is in the emotion and colour of the former and the soullessness of the latter.

It would be the same if some unfortunate child were taught to speak through a vocalised computer. The words would be understandable, but would lack all the attributes of tone and expression learned from imitating a human voice.

I was told of a couple who had enthusiastically chosen Suzuki violin training for their daughter, starting classes shortly after her fourth birthday. Two years later Fiona's mother was telling her sister-in-law, who had come on a weekend visit, of her daughter's remarkable progress.

'Do you have to buy the sheet music for the pieces she's trying to learn?' her guest enquired. 'I believe they're quite expensive.'

'Oh no,' Fiona's mother replied. 'She doesn't read music.'

'So she's really musically illiterate!'

'If you wish to think so,' Fiona's mother smiled, 'but that's no hindrance. The teacher says that she'll pick up reading quite easily in next year's classes. In six months she will read music.'

Then Fiona was told to pick up her violin and give a little recital. She played some variations on *Twinkle, twinkle* and a Bach minuet, with all the assurance of a confident expert.

This incident reminded me of the oft-told joke (professional musicians have a wealth of humorous anecdotes) about a veteran bass viol player who was asked whether his bad eyesight made it hard for him to sight-read in difficult symphonies.

'I don't sight-read,' the musician replied, 'anyway, not enough to spoil my playing.'

This exaggeration points to a fundamental truth. Familiarity and memory are more important than the ability to obey instructions on a sheet of music. Professional soloists give their recitals without a music stand in front of them. They play from memory.

The matter of learning to read music is the most usual criticism from parents investigating the possibilities of Suzuki teaching. They may have accepted the idea that a very young child can be taught because they have read about Suzuki's success and have seen mere tots playing with real skill. But their memories of musical education in their own youth influence them to believe that the first step is to 'learn the names of the notes' and practise simple scales.

A little thought will show that musical notation in a sort of code is a comparatively modern development in the history of music. In early times all music was handed down aurally from one generation to another, as folk music still is. The preservation of melodies, the origins of which are lost in the mists of time, shows how effective imitation without any written instruction can be.

If a child is instructed to read a note and play it, his concentration is divided. He will have to stare at the unfamiliar signs on a sheet of paper on a music stand or on a blackboard. He will have to concentrate on the signs and do so at the expense of forgetting all he has learned about posture and the correct holding of violin and bow. The desirable relaxed attitude will be in jeopardy and his memory of the tune he has rehearsed and memorised will be impaired.

The discipline inherent in playing any musical instrument is almost unconsciously observed when a child accurately imitates what he has heard properly rendered. The precision and accuracy come from his physical and mental experience combined with regular practice. He is unaware that he is in fact playing a piece in which, if the speed is, say, one crotchet a second, then a quaver lasts half a second, and a semiquaver lasts a quarter of a second.

When these are blended in a musical passage, the rhythm is pleasing to the ear. If a young child has to produce this rhythm from a musical score, never having previously heard it, he naturally finds it very difficult, no matter how much instruction he has received on the meaning of the signs.

Parents who remain convinced that reading music must be the foundation of playing it, should consider the ingenuity and inevitable difficulty used to set down all the emotional and colourful facets of music in the practical and cold-blooded signs on a paper. A note, lasting a fraction of a second, may be printed with at least half a dozen instructions, and often more. They will indicate whether the note is sharp or flat, the time signature, a different dynamic, an octave change, a tempo sign, and so on.

Pupils are disheartened by the difficulty of trying to read the notes and play them at the same time, which is the custom in conventional training after the first few lessons. How many adults can recall wrestling with this exercise and giving up because they found it too hard?

It seems better to learn to read notes and sing them (which is a modification in some methods of teaching) and then learn to handle the instrument; but in the opinion of Suzuki teachers, best of all is to leave reading for a year or so. By then the pupil will have mastered playing technique, and memorised a considerable number of pieces. He can then tackle the difficult feat of decoding a pattern based on five staff lines, reading along them from left to right as well as up and down, absorbing the instructions contained in the marks of notes and the ancillary words, letters and signs. He must learn to read the music with great rapidity, yet also check that his movements are correct.

'Surely,' parents of prospective Suzuki pupils will say, 'reading music must be taught at some stage or a pupil will never be able to play a piece he has never heard. He won't be able to play in any combination when there is a conductor constantly referring to the sheet music.'

Of course they learn to read – or in reality teach themselves with a little help from the teacher. The usual time is when a pupil reaches Books 3 or 4, the precise time depending on the teacher's assessment of the individual pupil's progress: whether the correct posture is being automatically adopted, whether his movements are easy and correct and his powers of imitating strong and accurate. Also important are signs that the pupil is showing interest in reading and asking questions about the symbols on sheet music. If any of these factors are undeveloped the teacher will probably postpone reading instruction. In any event, she will proceed quite slowly; two or three years will be the time a pupil may take to learn to read well enough to pick up a piece of music never previously seen or heard and sing a few phrases almost as easily as reading a sentence in a book.

The teacher will usually begin by distributing the sheet music for one of the pieces learned during the early lessons, with which, of course, the children are thoroughly familiar. She will explain that each letter stands for a group of notes – A flat, A natural, A sharp, and so on, with their appropriate finger placings. Pupils are shown where these notes appear on the music sheet and the first few bars of the familiar piece are played while they look at the sheet music. All children love puzzles, and are intrigued to discover that it is quite easy to name a note by observing where it occurs on the stave.

Reading music is used by many teachers in various games. A most effective one is for a teacher to draw three notes on a blackboard or card and to ask what word they spell: cab, add, dad, bad, bag, bed, egg, beg, cabbage, and so on. (This is a good game for the child to play at home.)

A more active game is to chalk the staff on an uncarpeted floor, on a scale large enough for a child's foot to be placed between the lines. The teacher calls a note by name, or plays it on a piano, and one by one the children move into the appropriate position on the stave. If the number of pupils is large enough, the teacher may place the children in positions of the notes of part of a piece they know well, and ask them to identify it without hearing it.

The old children's game of 'Simon says' can be a further aid to music reading. It can be adapted for three or four children, or for a score of them. 'Simon says Nicola must move to C,' and Nicola does so. 'Michael,

stand on E,' and if Michael moves without Simon saying
so he is out, as is any child who moves to the wrong place.
The culprits are brought in later, but don't score as much
as the note-perfect entrants.

The position of the notes is learned as quickly as
children of this age learn to read letters; they soon come
to accept that this is better than printing a mass of letters
up and down the stave and across it. Matching the note
signs with the sounds they produce in a familiar tune
becomes automatic.

Then they become curious about the signs and slightly
different appearance of the notes. The teacher may call
out the various terms while each child plays the notes
and observes them on the music sheet. Pupils will also be
told the meaning of actual words (mostly Italian) which
appear alongside the notes. While this stage may be a
challenge to the teacher, the pupils' curiosity and
fascination with this elaboration of the basic note code
will invariably ensure that her explanation is memorised,
thanks to the proof of their essential place in music
reading which comes from their own playing.

Once a pupil appears to have solved the details of this
fascinating puzzle, the teacher will test his knowledge by
giving him a piece of music he has not previously played.
This is essential, because with a piece the pupil knows by
heart and can play perfectly, he may look at the music
but will not really absorb the significance of the
markings.

Pressure to develop sight-reading ability is always
slow and gentle. It is an intellectual accomplishment
which the pupil may feel is a hindrance to the activity he
has learned to love – playing music. The teacher will
therefore usually make reading just part of the lesson
and not a special occasion. After all, even in ordinary
reading, it may take the most precocious child some time
to learn to read more than simple words and sentences.

After the first enthusiasm to 'break the code' a pupil will feel that reading music is boring and a needless extra, since he can play quite well without understanding all those additional instructions printed on the page of music. Parents who have little or no knowledge of playing an instrument are sometimes unconscious culprits in allowing this attitude to persist. Perhaps mother has kept up her own efforts to play her own violin, or dad demonstrates that he can strum out a tune on the piano without ever having learned a note. In effect they are opting out from the parent-teacher relationship which is so important to support Suzuki teaching. This is a pity, for their child is on the threshold of becoming an accomplished instrumentalist.

When a child joins a group of his peers to participate in a concert or large class, he will be at a disadvantage in tackling a piece he has hitherto not heard if he cannot sight-read. He will not be able to understand the instructions of teacher or conductor. He will be at a dead end, thoroughly capable of playing all the pieces he has heard but finding it difficult or impossible to play new pieces which attract him and which would enable him to amass a real repertoire.

A few children abandon Suzuki classes at this stage, partly because they are temperamentally unsuited to serious study, but much more frequently through lack of home support. The belief that Suzuki produces infant prodigies dies hard. The skilful playing of five and six year-olds is only a stage of their potential ability. It is almost tragic if teaching ceases so soon – a waste of money and, more importantly, of a child's hopes. This temporary crisis, when it exists, needs firm encouragement from both teacher and parents to master the difficulty of reading. The child can be helped by having a tape of his own playing to compare with that of his teacher or a professional. He will realise that, with reading skill, he will be able to produce those embellishments of playing, such as the duration of note, phrasing, tempo and so on, which he has hitherto omitted.

When he has the music sheet in front of him, he will be able to see that the improvements he has made are duly described by signs and words on the stave. Pitch, timing, form, style and expression will be added to his increasing technique. 'You played that very well,' the teacher may say. 'Can you do so again?' Without the ability to read, the quality which impressed the teacher may have been partly a happy accident. If it was the result of following the music signs he will be able to repeat it.

In Suzuki's words, understanding reading is not enough. Under his methods it is the secondary part of any lesson. In general, pupils first play a few pieces with which they are thoroughly familiar and enjoy, without reference to the sheet music, and the lesson ends with a further period of playing music unsighted. Only a proportion of the time between these two activities is devoted to reading music.

The aim is to enable the pupil to gain a good grasp of a piece of music merely by reading it, so that eventually he can absorb the messages of the printed signs and hear the music in his head. This will take some years, by which time the pupil could be studying Book 6 onwards.

At this age some pupils show interest in other instruments, and parents often enquire if the earlier training on the violin can be profitably adapted for other instruments. A popular preference is one of the other instruments in the violin family, especially the 'cello. Most of the teaching of violin playing in the first two years or so will pave the way to learning the 'cello, but the pupil must obviously be big enough to handle this larger instrument. Smaller versions of the standard 'cello are available, but it is a fact that not all Suzuki teachers are willing to teach it.

However, if a pupil shows real interest in learning to play the 'cello it would be wrong to dismiss the idea. 'Cellists are in demand in both amateur and professional groups and orchestras. As with the violin, it is hardly ever too early to start learning, given that physical development is adequate. Rostropovitch, the world's greatest living 'cellist, began to learn at the age of seven, taught by his father.

If the pupil chooses the viola, he can adapt to it quite easily, as the fingering is roughly the same; only the tuning of the strings is different (C,G,D,A, as opposed to G,D,A,E). Viola music is mainly written in the alto clef, but the treble clef has to be learned as well, so it will be an advantage to have already learned music reading.

Learning to play the piano by Suzuki methods begins, as with violin lessons, by listening, in order to develop the memory. The first pieces are learned by trial and error repetition. The teacher will sit beside the child, paying close attention to the physical factors of a loose arm, flexible wrist and firm fingers. The need for this individual tuition makes it usual for piano teaching to be given as a private lesson. With more than one pupil, all but one have to sit around just listening. By its very structure, with black and white keys controlling each note, reading music often begins earlier than with violin teaching. Usually reading the music starts during study of Book 2.

An advantage in deciding on piano lessons rather than starting on the violin is that piano playing is socially popular among all classes and ages. It is also one of the easiest instruments to learn to play (although that does not necessarily include playing well!). In a household where a well-tuned piano exists, and private lessons can be afforded, it could well be a good choice for a child's musical education. It may not, however, be easy to find a teacher trained in the Suzuki method of piano tuition. In any event, the parents' role will be even greater than in the case of violin tuition. One parent will be expected to be able to read music and to assist in teaching the child to do so.

10   Playing in Concert

Public interest in Suzuki Talent Education has stemmed from pictures of small children – usually Japanese – playing on their violins with all the confidence and much of the skill of adult professionals. The usual TV presentation is by children aged from six to ten, in groups of twenty or thirty. Although they may make world-wide tours, they are not, of course, professional players. Accompanied by parents or guardians, these children regard selection for public appearances as a reward. Like all children, they are not averse to the chance of showing off

Some of the Suzuki children's concerts are intended to prove that all children can benefit from Suzuki methods. In a huge Tokyo gymnasium, concerts have been given by an orchestra of a thousand child violinists.

Before his death, the famous 'cellist Pablo Casals attending a Suzuki children's concert at which four hundred children played in unison variations on *Twinkle, twinkle*, followed by a Vivaldi concerto and the Bach concerto written for two violins, but in this case played by four hundred. Casals said afterwards it had been one of the most moving scenes that one could experience.

Mass performances of this kind are, of course, good for publicity, but Suzuki's main purpose is to prove that skilled performance is not the exception with a few gifted children, but is the rule. It is reflected in the vast number of recitals given by ten or twenty children, sometimes just for parents, relatives and friends, sometimes as a local musical attraction in a theatre or concert hall. Some sort of public or semi-public performance will certainly provide visible and audible proof that a child has gained confidence as well as skill. The first appearance will assuredly be just one of many.

Group practices are the preliminary stages. If the teacher has more than one class of just a few children who are given regular – probably weekly – lessons, she may, once a month, have a group lesson with children from two or three classes. These group occasions are valuable in eradicating shyness, and they help to develop musicianship – playing in harmony, keeping time, and playing as well as the other children. The teacher, while having the opportunity to identify faults by comparison of one child with another, will adopt the role of a conductor familiarising the children with instruction at each stage of rehearsing a piece of music.

A feature of group playing which is invariably noticed is how much the children enjoy it, partly as a change from lessons which they have probably had at weekly intervals for eighteen months or two years, but also because they make new friends.

This is particularly valuable in the case of a child who has no brothers or sisters and is accustomed to amusements of a solitary kind. Playing music is essentially a social activity. When a professional soloist shuts himself away and practises for hours on end, he is always envisaging an audience. Once a child has enjoyed playing in a larger group than usual he will do the same.

He will learn that the need to give an error-free rendering is much greater when others around him are playing correctly than when he is playing solo. His sensitive hearing will tell him that a split-second error in timing or a wrong note can spoil the entire group's performance, whereas, when he was playing alone it was hardly noticeable. Awareness of this produces a sense of personal responsibility and self-discipline.

Suzuki insists that his pupils should perform in the presence of others – not only the mothers, teacher and the other pupils – as frequently as possible. He has found that children react positively to the challenge of having comparative strangers listening to them, and do not feel embarrassed.

Observing a class of young children playing before an audience is a stimulating and interesting experience. On the first occasion there may be an outburst of jitters or a tendency to giggle. This is before the children begin to play. They soon settle down quietly and concentrate on getting everything right.

Once children have experienced the thrill and satisfaction of playing in concert to an audience, which will certainly have shown its approval, they become so engrossed in their performance at subsequent appearances that they are unaffected by any untoward noise or disturbance in the hall, although afterwards they will mention that it was a pity it occurred. This shows that they were aware of the environment as well as the need to play well. They are learning that they can influence the thoughts and reactions of adults simply through the power of their musical performance.

At any concert given by children, there will inevitably be some parents trying to attract the attention of their child on the stage. This is understandable but should be avoided. The child will have spotted where his parents are sitting. He knows that they are eager for him to do well and are silently encouraging him, but he hopes fervently that they won't 'show him up' by some fussy gesture.

He can certainly do without any distraction of this kind, needing all his concentration for playing. He can be praised afterwards, and if anything went wrong he can be reassured, so that he will have the encouragement to do better next time.

There are naturally some exceptions to most children's trouble-free acceptance of playing with a group in public; invariably, as already mentioned, these are to be found in one-child families. It can be disheartening when such a child plays well at his classes and during practices at home, but goes to pieces when watched by strangers. This crisis needs careful and sympathetic handling, minimising but not ignoring the all-too obvious failure, while reassuring the child that he has nothing to dread because he really can play as well as the other children, and better than many of them. A successful approach like this will forestall real problems, such as the child refusing to practise at home and saying he hates going to his class.

Some mothers can be at their wit's end in trying to deal with the difficulty, not knowing the best way to solve it. I know of one group of parents with children at a large class who formed a mutual help organisation, known to the half dozen members as Suzukis Anonymous, which has proved highly successful. Telephone numbers are exchanged so that an exasperated mother can ring a fellow member with such questions as, 'David doesn't want to practise this afternoon. Has Susan ever acted up like this?'

Invariably the reply is, 'Yes; now and then, and long before there was this public appearance challenge.'

'What did you do?'

Between them they work out a sensible solution, and the risk of a child dropping out, after all the months of training, disappears.

A teacher has told me about another group of parents who became so interested in musical performances that they formed a small ensemble and revived their half-forgotten ability to play a piano and some stringed instruments. They practised regularly enough to play a few pieces passably well and were offered the chance to contribute to a Christmas-time concert at the local school, more or less as a novelty item, billed as 'the Suzuki parents quintet'.

Two of the amateur musicians began to hint at excuses to avoid playing. But these would-be defectors saw their children's disappointment and went ahead. I was told that it was wryly amusing to overhear a small child, after the concert was over, say that Daddy was 'really very good', thus reversing the usual parent-child role.

This development of a practical interest in music among parents of Suzuki pupils is not unusual, thanks to the stress laid on parental participation in the educational programme.

A happy ending story concerns twins, Emma and Jonathan. Their parents were not really interested in music beyond liking to have the family transistor switched on to the current pop hits for background entertainment.

It was not until the twins were five years old and had started school that the parents even heard the name Suzuki. Emma came home one day to say that one of the teachers gave violin lessons and her new schoolfriend Helen had started to learn to play the violin. Her mum and dad had asked for her to be taught in the special class held on Saturday mornings.

Jonathan, determined not to be left out of this fascinating side of school life, said he had passed a classroom and had seen a boy playing a big instrument called a 'cello, and that was what he would like to learn.

Their parents duly made enquiries. The music teacher explained that Jonathan was on the small side for handling such a large instrument as a 'cello. However, he seemed a strong and determined boy, and there was every reason to see how he would get on, with the assurance that his growth ought to keep up with his musical progress. Regarding Emma, there was no problem. The teacher could arrange for the loan of an instrument, just to see if the children really wanted to be taught. She outlined the cost of instruments if the parents decided to enroll the twins on the Suzuki course.

The parents rather hesitantly agreed. They were fortunately willing to bear the expense of two instruments, the fees, and the other costs, so long as they felt that they were a real investment in their children's future.

Both Emma and Jonathan made exceptionally good progress in the first two years of their Suzuki tuition. As so frequently occurs with twins, each child vied with the other to succeed. They did in fact make more rapid progress than any of their fellow-pupils. For their parents, the teacher's encouraging reports and the pleasure of seeing the twins receiving applause at end-of-term concerts aroused mixed feelings. They were naturally proud of the twins' success, but were beset with a sense of their own inadequacy. They confessed to the teacher that they felt guilty about their failure to recognise inborn talent until, by accident, Emma had come home with the story of her friend's lesson and Jonathan had talked about the boy playing the 'cello.

The teacher told the familiar story of Suzuki's basic creed: talent is not an accident of birth. It is dormant in every new-born baby. The sooner it is helped to emerge the better, but it is not too late to make up for lost time once the truth of talent as a birthright is accepted.

Recognition of this truth gradually changed the parents' attitude to music. The father began to buy cassettes and records of pieces the teacher had mentioned. He found he was deriving genuine pleasure from listening to instrumental soloists and classical orchestral pieces, almost unconsciously developing discrimination and good taste.

The mother, who had a quite delightful voice but confined her singing to snatches of the latest pop number as she carried out her household chores, took the plunge and applied to join the local choral society. Rather to her surprise, the chorus master told her she had a pleasant mezzo-soprano voice, a good ear for pitch and tone, and that he would be happy to have her attend rehearsals. She is now a full member of the society, singing in combined choirs which have been engaged for TV concerts.

The side-effects of Suzuki Talent Education for children in improving their parents' awareness of its contribution to family life are invariably experienced after two or three years of tuition.

Mothers who have occasionally been tempted to feel that the constant supervision of practising and attending classes is becoming a burden, change their minds as audible and visual results of their children's education become obvious. Fathers who have had some difficulty in concealing their annoyance that the living room was regularly turned into a music studio, cease their tendency to complain that every activity, when they come home from work or want to enjoy a week-end break, is thwarted. Perhaps, to their surprise, they find they are becoming fascinated by the whole business of music.

The hope that a youngster will really want to play before an audience can be realised by the stimulation of attending live recitals with the whole family. Accurate as recordings now are, excellent as TV and radio concert programmes may be, they are only substitutes for the live performance at which the audience in effect participates in the music. Every professional knows that there is a great difference between playing to an empty auditorium during a rehearsal and performing before a full house. Taking children to see a live concert will stimulate their desire to play in the limelight, quite apart from the information they absorb from watching professionals, whether they are soloists or orchestral players.

Really enthusiastic parents know that a little effort helps to widen the scope of public performances once their children are capable of playing in groups. They do not leave it all to the teacher or wait for enquiries. Many small events can be discovered by contacting a variety of organisations concerned with the social life of a district.

Old folks' homes, Darby and Joan clubs, children's homes and some hospitals need entertainment which will not involve expense and will provide a short interlude of pleasure for people deprived of much contrast in their lives. Many churches regularly hold recitals, not necessarily of sacred music. Women's Institutes, Townswomen's Guild's, and Mothers' Union branches readily include items in their regular meetings when the teacher and some of the mothers describe Suzuki tuition and include a performance by a few Suzuki pupils.

Any public performance, whether the audience consists of a dozen people or several hundred, is good for the child's self-esteem. He will feel he is getting somewhere, and will be stimulated to work harder at his lessons. Experience has shown that this is just what he needs after about three years of tuition, when he may be prone to think he knows everything. It is the stage when dropouts occur; this is both a waste of past effort and a failure on the part of the parents to realise the child's real potential, not only as a violin player but as a young human being who knows that he can, with persistence, succeed in any field of human activity that eventually becomes his lifetime's ambition.

11 The Suzuki System:
Your Questions Answered

We have two children, a boy and a girl. Both show a great interest in music, and there have been quite well-known professionals on both sides of the family in the past. Would Suzuki training be the best type if a career in music is envisaged, and what are the chances of making a living?

As recorded in these pages, Suzuki always stresses that his system of Talent Education is not intended to produce professional musicians. Nevertheless, any Suzuki pupil who completes the course has at least three years' start over those trained by traditional methods. Suzuki pupils adapt without trouble to the educational system and routine in colleges of music.

A career as a professional musician involves competition in making a steady living exceeded only by that in the acting profession. Many would-be professional players eventually take up teaching. So far as opportunities are available, violinists probably stand the best chance of orchestral work, simply because an orchestra usually employs up to twenty violinists. Viola players and 'cellists are also in demand. The piano, as a solo instrument, requires outstanding talent but admittedly with comparable rewards.

Thoughts of a career for either or both of your children should be left until they are at least in early adolescence. Their teacher will be able to assess whether they have exceptional ability and the strength of character to persist. In earlier years their expressed ambition may be little more than a passing whim. In any event, no parent should try to drive a young child to choose an adult career fifteen years ahead, destroying the pleasure of learning to play music for music's sake.

Our hope is that our four year-old son will learn the piano. Both my husband and myself play the piano moderately well. Would there be any point in learning the violin simply to drop it and change to the piano?

Suzuki's system applies to teaching the piano, but it may not be easy to find a teacher with this specialised experience. Learning to play the violin would be easier for a four year-old and the lessons would stand him in good stead when learning to read music, which is really essential for a pianist.

All the information I have read about Suzuki training stresses the need for one parent to participate in a child's practising at home. Does this have to continue right through the course of violin lessons?

No. After three or four years a youngster is mature enough to practise by himself, which does not mean that interest in his progress and being on hand to praise and criticise should be only an occasional parental contribution.

Children like to be rewarded for anything they do well. Does Suzuki advocate a reward?

He believes in giving praise after a child's lesson or home practice, but this should not be so uncritical that it sounds false even to a child. 'Yes, you can play that piece,' he is reported to have said to a boy whose efforts had been a near-failure, 'now, let's see if you can't improve it.' He did not tell the boy he had played well when he hadn't.

As regards a reward, if it must be given, Suzuki suggests that it should be presented before the practice session, and not after it.

Nothing I have read about learning the violin says anything about a left-handed child. Doesn't that preclude any chance of my child succeeding?

Playing the violin involves both hands. The movements involved are not those made naturally in day-to-day activities. With the exception of a physical handicap in the right arm, a child who is left-handed when it comes to writing, drawing, catching a ball, and so on – all one-arm activities – will find no problem in using both arms when playing a violin or, for that matter, any other instrument requiring two hands.

Can accompanying a child to the lessons be shared between husband and wife or with the parent of another pupil?

Ideally, one parent should be the sole participant in the lessons; either mother or father (quite a number of fathers do take on this role, especially if the weekly class is on a Saturday), but not alternately, since this will confuse the child and make it difficult for one parent to know all that occurred at the previous lessons. A friendly neighbour with a child who is also a pupil is acceptable, providing the children like each other, on those occasions when unavoidable duties mean that the only alternative is to miss the lesson. But a regular routine of one mother one week and the other the next will not be approved by the teacher.

Can two children of different ages both start learning at the same time?

Certainly. It is quite a usual practice, when two children of the same family have an age gap of two years or so. With proper tuition, the progress of each child will show hardly any difference.

Is it possible to calculate the cost of Suzuki violin training? It would obviously be wrong to embark on a course of lessons without knowing what expenses are involved.

There is no gainsaying that, over the years of a complete course, costs will be considerable. It is just possible that the actual tuition will be provided gratis by the local education authority as part of the school's teaching services. Private lessons are about £5 for a half-hour class, with £10 per term for weekly sessions in groups.

The initial costs include buying a miniature violin or hiring one: £40–£50 for purchase and around £35 for a year's hire, plus, possibly, a violin (preferably hired) for the parent to learn the basics of playing; a tape recorder and player, if not already possessed; the Suzuki Books (often cheaper when obtained from the teacher who may have sets used by previous pupils). Running costs are low: rosin, new strings, new bow hair, etc.

Neither my husband nor myself has any ability to play a musical instrument. We have only rarely listened to a classical concert on TV or radio. Won't this mean that our children would have such a poor example that they could not really benefit from Suzuki teaching?

Give your children the opportunity to hear good music as early in their lives as you can, and there will be no problem, either for them or for you as parents.

12 The Language of Music Terms

Some parents are likely to be perplexed by music terms which they hear and read, as will their children. Most of the words are of Italian origin, difficult to understand without an explanation, but easy to remember.

Below are some of the terms they will come across once their child moves to more advanced lessons and reads music; the teacher will probably use them for instruction and explanation.

Accelerando	Gradually increasing in speed.
Accent	Stress falling on the principal beats in a bar. Notes to be more than normally stressed carry the signs > or – above them.
Adagio	Slowly and leisurely.
Affettuoso	Tenderly.
Affrettando	Quickening of the tempo.
Allargando	Slower and fuller in tone.
Allegro	Briskly.
Amoroso	Lovingly.
Andante	Moderately slow time.
Animato	Lively.
Arpeggio	Notes of a chord played in quick succession.
A tempo	Resume original pace.
Au talon	Use heel of bow.

Bar	Vertical line across stave on printed music dividing the piece into sections of equal time value.
Beat	Unit of time measurement.
Brio	With spirit and liveliness.
Calando	Slower and softer.
Cedez	Instruction to play more slowly.
Chord	Group of notes sounded together.
Clef	Sign at beginning of stave to indicate pitch.
Coll' arco	Use bow again after pizzicato passage.
Con moto	Quickly.
Crescendo	Play gradually more loudly, indicated by sign $<$.
Da capo	Go back again to the beginning of the piece.
Diminuendo	Becoming gradually softer, shown by sign $>$.
Dolce	Sweetly.
Forte	Loudly, shown as *f*.
Fortissimo	Very loudly, shown as *ff.*
Glissando	Sliding finger up or down the violin string instead of fingering the notes separately; drawing finger, nail downwards, rapidly over piano keys.
Incalcando	Louder and faster.
Largo	Slowly and expansively.
Legato	Smoothly, one note joined to the next.
Lento	Slowly.
Molto	Very, as allegro molto: very fast.
Non tanto	Not too much – instruction not to be too rigid in observing sign or word regarding tempo, etc.
Open note	Note produced by open string where other notes are made by placing finger on string.

Piano	Softly, Shown as *p*.
Pianissimo	Very softly. Shown as *pp*.
Pizzicato	Playing strings, normally bowed, by plucking with the fingers.
Presto	Quickly.
Prestissimo	Very quickly.
Rallentando	Getting gradually slower. Shown as *rall*.
Slur	Curved line over a group of notes to indicate phrasing.
Spiccato	Notes produced by bouncing the bow on the string.
Staccato	Playing a note briefly and detached from the following note, indicated by a dot over the note.
Stave (staff)	Five horizontal lines on which music is written.
Stop	Pressing down the string with the finger to shorten the vibrating length and thus produce a higher note than on an open string.
Tremolo	Quickly repeating a note or notes by agitating the bow or rapid stopping on the finger board.
Una corda	Instruction to play the piano with the 'soft' pedal depressed.
Vibrato	Rapid fluctuation in pitch produced by slight rocking of the finger on the violin string.
Vivace	Lively and quickly.

Music to Play to your Child

Throughout this book it has been stressed that while classical music is not the only type you should play to your child, it is, nevertheless, the best to choose, and Suzuki himself advocates classical music. In case your knowledge of the classical repertoire is limited, or if you are unsure which pieces would be most suitable, here are a few that you may like to try. They are all well-tried favourites with an established general appeal.

Record companies change their lists with startling rapidity, and therefore it has been felt best not to recommend actual recordings. The pieces listed below should, however, be generally available and any reputable record shop will advise you on a good recording.

For the very young child

Badinerie from the Suite No 2 by Bach	This is a flute solo and is a lively and tuneful piece.
The second movement from the Clarinet Quintet by Mozart	A glorious slow tune which is warm and secure. Very suitable for those quiet, peaceful moments.
The second movement from the Trumpet Concerto in E flat by Haydn	A trumpet playing a smooth, yet rhythmical tune. If you want something more lively, try the last movement.

'The Swan' from *The Carnival of the Animals* by Saint-Saëns

The 'cello is the soloist here. It is one of the most beautiful short pieces for the 'cello. It can usually be obtained in a 'cello and piano version, as well as the original where the 'cello is accompanied by the orchestra.

Bagatelle – *Für Elise* by Beethoven

Even if you do not recognise the title, you will remember the the tune when you hear it. This is for solo piano.

Serenade from the String Quartet Opus 3 No 5 in F by Haydn

A beautiful violin solo accompanied by pizzicato strings. Again, this is a tune which you will recognise as soon as you hear it.

Chanson de Matin by Elgar

For violin and piano. Quite short and not at all over-sentimental.

Humoresque in G flat major Opus 101 by Dvořák

Originally a piano solo, it has been arranged for violin and piano. It is one of Suzuki's pieces in Book 3.

Caprice Viennois by Kreisler

Written by one of the most famous violinists of the first half of this century, this piece is greatly loved by all violinists who have the technique to play it.

Minuet from *Berenice* by Handel

This is part of the overture to Handel's opera of this name. It is popular with string orchestras in particular, as a fill-in when the main recording is insufficient to make up a full record or tape.

For the older child

The pieces below do not necessarily replace those in the previous list, but include orchestral pieces as well as solos.

'Alla Marcia' from *The Karelia Suite* by Sibelius	A most catchy tune with plenty of rhythm to set the foot tapping.
Eine Kleine Nachtmusik by Mozart	You can take any part or movement of this and you will find it tuneful and interesting.
Overture from *Hansel and Gretel* by Humperdinck	This is a well-written overture and the opera itself is based on a story not unlike our *Babes in the Wood*.
Radetzky March by Johann Strauss	Immediately appealing and much in the style of this composer's more famous waltzes.
March from *The Love of Three Oranges* by Prokofiev	Another march, but in a modern and very catchy style.
Polonaise in A major Opus 40 No 1 by Chopin	A very exciting piano piece.
Simple Symphony by Benjamin Britten	A short work for string orchestra. Try the 'Boisterous Bourrée' and the 'Playful Pizzicato'.
Peer Gynt Suite by Grieg	There is every mood here. Try 'Morning' for a peaceful time and 'In the Hall of the Mountain King' for something more lively and exciting.
'Claire de Lune' from *Suite Bergamasque* by Debussy	A piano solo creating a mood of peace and tranquillity.

Polka from *The Bartered Bride* by Smetana	An exciting dance, full of rhythms to get you dancing, too.
Fantasia on *Greensleeves* by Vaughan Williams	A good entry into the more classical use of folk music, based on one of England's best known folk songs.

These lists have no magical properties, nor are they in any way exhaustive or exclusive, but they may help you in getting started. It must be pointed out, however, that children's tastes differ enormously; while these pieces have proved successful with children in the past, it cannot be guaranteed that your own child will enjoy them all. Be guided by his obvious preferences and use them as a starting point for subsequent choices.

Useful Addresses

The British Suzuki Institute, 21 London Road, St Albans, Herts, AL1 1LQ. Although there are not as yet official Suzuki groups in Britain, the Hon Secretary of the Association can provide particulars of classes in many areas.

Details of musical associations, societies and groups of both national and regional status in Britain, are listed in the *British Music Year Book*, available in all larger public reference libraries. It is published by Classical Music Magazine, 52, Floral Street, London, WC2E 9DA.

The Incorporated Society of Musicians' *Register of Private Teachers* is distributed annually to all public libraries. Teachers are listed under type of instrument taught and by area. In case of difficulty, write to the Society at 10, Stratford Place, London, W1N 9AE. From the same address, the National Federation of Music Societies issues names and addresses of local amateur musical groups.

The Schools Music Association, 4, Newman Road, Bromley, Kent, maintains lists of schools which organise recitals, concerts, etc., by pupils.

Musical instrument and music shops are listed in the Yellow Pages of the telephone directory.

Further Reading

Nurtured by Love, Shinichi Suzuki. Exposition Press.

The Suzuki Concept, Edited by Elizabeth Mills and Therese Cecile Murphy. Diablo Press.

In the Suzuki Style, Elizabeth Mills. Diablo Press. (The above books are published in the USA. Suzuki teachers may be able to supply copies).

A Parents' Guide to the Suzuki Method, Alina Thornton. (Music Sales Pty Ltd in Australia and Music Sales Corporation as UK distributors).

Young Children Learning, Barbara Tizard and Martin Hughes. Fontana Books.

Kindergarten is Too Late, Masaru Ibuka. Souvenir Press and Sphere Books.

You Can Teach Your Child Intelligence, David Lewis. Souvenir Press.

The Secret Language of Your Child, David Lewis. Souvenir Press.

How to be a Gifted Parent, David Lewis. Souvenir Press.

Fontana Paperbacks: Non-fiction

Fontana is a leading paperback publisher of non-fiction. Below are some recent titles.

☐ THE LIVING PLANET David Attenborough £8.95
☐ SCOTLAND'S STORY Tom Steel £4.95
☐ HOW TO SHOOT AN AMATEUR NATURALIST Gerald Durrell £2.25
☐ THE ENGLISHWOMAN'S HOUSE
  Alvilde Lees-Milne and Derry Moore £7.95
☐ BRINGING UP CHILDREN ON YOUR OWN Liz McNeill Taylor £2.50
☐ WITNESS TO WAR Charles Clements £2.95
☐ IT AIN'T NECESSARILY SO Larry Adler £2.95
☐ BACK TO BASICS Mike Nathenson £2.95
☐ POPPY PARADE Arthur Marshall (ed.) £2.50
☐ LEITH'S COOKBOOK
  Prudence Leith and Caroline Waldegrave £5.95
☐ HELP YOUR CHILD WITH MATHS Alan T. Graham £2.95
☐ TEACH YOUR CHILD TO READ Peter Young and Colin Tyre £2.95
☐ BEDSIDE SEX Richard Huggett £2.95
☐ GLEN BAXTER, HIS LIFE Glen Baxter £4.95
☐ LIFE'S RICH PAGEANT Arthur Marshall £2.50
☐ H FOR 'ENRY Henry Cooper £3.50
☐ THE SUPERWOMAN SYNDROME Marjorie Hansen Shaevitz £2.50
☐ THE HOUSE OF MITFORD Jonathan and Catherine Guinness £5.95
☐ ARLOTT ON CRICKET David Rayvern Allen (ed.) £3.50
☐ THE QUALITY OF MERCY William Shawcross £3.95
☐ AGATHA CHRISTIE Janet Morgan £3.50

You can buy Fontana paperbacks at your local bookshop or newsagent. Or you can order them from Fontana Paperbacks, Cash Sales Department, Box 29, Douglas, Isle of Man. Please send a cheque, postal or money order (not currency) worth the purchase price plus 15p per book for postage (maximum postage required is £3).

NAME (Block letters) _____

ADDRESS _____

_____

_____

While every effort is made to keep prices low, it is sometimes necessary to increase them at short notice. Fontana Paperbacks reserve the right to show new retail prices on covers which may differ from those previously advertised in the text or elsewhere.